PATHFINDER

ADVENTURE PATH ✷ PART 3 of 6

Rise of the Runelords:
THE HOOK MOUNTAIN MASSACRE

CREDITS

Editor-in-Chief • James Jacobs
Art Director • Sarah E. Robinson
Associate Editor • F. Wesley Schneider
Assistant Editor • James L. Sutter
Editorial Assistance • Mike McArtor
Managing Art Director • James Davis
Production Manager • Jeff Alvarez
Brand Manager • Jason Bulmahn
Marketing Director • Joshua J. Frost
Publisher • Erik Mona

Cover Artist
Wayne Reynolds

Cartographer
Rob Lazzaretti

Contributing Artists
Jeff Carlisle
John Gravato
Andrew Hou
Kyle Hunter
JZConcepts
Warren Mahy
Arnold Tsang
Ben Wootten

Contributing Authors
Nicolas Logue
Mike McArtor
James L. Sutter

Paizo CEO • Lisa Stevens
Corporate Accountant • Dave Erickson
Staff Accountant • Christopher Self
Technical Director • Vic Wertz
Director of Operations • Jeff Alvarez

Paizo Publishing, LLC
2700 Richards Road, Suite 201
Bellevue, WA 98005
paizo.com

TABLE OF CONTENTS

THE HILLS HAVE HOOKS

I have no one to blame but myself.

I knew going into this adventure what Nicolas Logue was like. I knew how deep his wells of perversion ran. Or at least I thought I did. When I contacted him to have him write "The Hook Mountain Massacre," I told him to write me an adventure featuring a tribe of ogres that were part fleshy-headed mutants (a la Wes Craven's classic *The Hills Have Eyes*), part degenerate inbred hillbillies, and part ravenous backwoods murderers. Oh, and if he could throw in a little bit of *The Blair Witch Project*, that'd be cool too.

Nick actually wrote this adventure at the center of a hurricane of activity that included getting married, moving from Hawaii to New York, writing half of *E1: Carnival of Tears* for our GameMastery Modules line, and preparing his transformation into the Iron DM M. C. for Gen Con. How he managed to churn out well over 50,000 words of backwoods horror and mutant hillbilly mayhem sort of boggles the mind, but here it is. I can't say if the state of his mind at the height of this vortex of activity had anything to do with some of the stuff he wove into "Hook Mountain Massacre," but if it did, I think I need to arrange for him to move across the country more often.

In any event, several months after I first asked Nick to write it, this manuscript was sitting in my inbox, violating my other emails and playing creepy banjo music. It was perfect.

Well, almost perfect. Nick went a little... over the top, shall we say, in places. A few of the scenes in his original draft were things I

can never unread. They've scarred parts of my mind that I thought, after growing up on a steady diet of Stephen King, Clive Barker, and John Carpenter, had been as traumatized as they could get. I was wrong. Even as I was cackling in glee to myself at what three not-so-lovely hags had in store for an unlucky commander of a remote mountain fort, or re-reading in disbelief what Jeppo Graul was doing to his brother Hograth when the PCs were scheduled to show up, the editor in the back of my mind was shaking his head. "You can't ever let *that* see print," he said. "The police would show up at Nick's house and take him away, and then he'd never be able to write adventures for you again!" It was, therefore, greed for future Logue adventures that spared you the atrocities and horrors of the uncut "Hook Mountain Massacre," not any misplaced sense of protection for delicate sensibilities out there among *Pathfinder* readers. I'd love to have exposed what this guy came up with to you all, but then he'd be taken away to the happy house and that'd be that. While Nick's arch-nemesis Richard Pett (himself quite the sicko—see "The Skinsaw Murders" for proof) would doubtlessly revel at the development, future *Pathfinders* and GameMastery Modules would be the poorer for Nick's relocation to an environment where sharp writing utensils aren't allowed.

I suspect I let a lot more of the warped and twisted stuff stay in the final adventure than I thought I would. The Grauls, for example... well... you'll see.

MOVIES AS INSPIRATION

First there was "The Skinsaw Murders" and its obvious inspiration from movies like *Se7en* and *Dawn of the Dead*. Now we have "The Hook Mountain Massacre," which certainly has its genesis among viewings of such fine films as *The Hills Have Eyes*, *Deliverance*, and of course, *The Texas Chainsaw Massacre*. Is this a bad thing? Is it somehow "less legitimate" than drawing inspiration from fantasy books? Would Gygax have listed "Recommended Movies" in Appendix N of the first edition *Dungeon Master's Guide* instead of "Recommended Reading" had he written it in the age of DVDs?

Written stories remain my own primary source of inspiration for creating RPG adventures and campaigns, and Gygax's Appendix N is certainly an exact shopping list of most of the books I turn to for ideas, but that doesn't mean that movies can't be as important when you're coming up with concepts for your own campaign. And despite my own preference for horror, you can extract great adventures from any genre of movie that inspires you. *King Kong* certainly inspired the creation of the classic adventures *Isle of Dread* and *Isle of the Ape*, the Hammer Horror movies left their mark on dozens of Ravenloft adventures, and the first page of the *Eberron Campaign Setting* has an excellent list of inspiring movies. Peter Jackson's version of *Return of the King* was certainly in my mind when I was writing *Red Hand of Doom*.

But what other kinds of adventures can you extract from movies? Certainly plots pulled from movies like *Beastmaster*, *Dragonslayer*, or *Conan the Barbarian* can serve as exciting adventures, but don't discount movies from genres beyond fantasy as sources of inspiration. Listed below are three movies that I count among my personal favorites and that I think could serve as the inspiration for some really memorable but unusual adventure plots.

Tarantula: Any of the giant insect movies from the '50s work here, but *Tarantula* remains my favorite. In this adventure, the PCs are called upon to help defend a small town against a Colossal spider running amok. The adventure works best if the PCs are low enough level that they can't defeat the spider in combat, but instead are forced to help evacuate a town and then discover some other way to defeat the spider, perhaps by luring it into a narrow canyon and engineering an avalanche to crush it.

Jurassic Park: In a world with magic and monsters, it's no real stretch of the imagination to envision a "monster park" populated by various deadly creatures all kept under control by some sort of magic (*charm monster*, anyone?). Of course, when the PCs come to visit, they'll have front-row seats for the carnage that ensues when a competing wizard sneaks in to steal the magic item that keeps all those monsters complacent and confined to their pens.

Aguirre, the Wrath of God: This classic Werner Herzog movie follows the fate of a doomed expedition of conquistidors in search of El Dorado. Certainly, there's been plenty of adventures where the PCs have to mount an expedition into the wilds to find a lost city, but an adventure based on this movie wouldn't ever reach that city—the city might not even exist. Instead, the PCs would be traipsing into the wilds following a leader who grows more and more insane, and eventually becomes the villain of the story. How the PCs handle an insane leader and then escape the perils of the deep jungle might be more exciting than just investigating yet another monster-haunted ruin on the edge of the map.

Of course, movies aren't the only source of insipiration we drew upon for Rise of the Runelords, and with next issue's "Fortress of the Stone Giants" you'll see a modern take on one of the most classic adventures of them all—the foray into the mountains to take up arms against the giants! Hope your PCs have some extra healing handy for this one!

James Jacobs
Editor-in-Chief
james.jacobs@paizo.com

THE HOOK MOUNTAIN MASSACRE

RISE OF THE RUNELORDS: CHAPTER THREE

When the hearth fires burn low in the dead of night, people whisper grim tales of Hook Mountain, of degenerate clans of ogres, of malformed and inbred giants notorious for their rusty hooks, of jewelry harvested from the bodies of their victims, and of horrific lusts. Parents frighten naughty children with stories of the Hook Mountain ogres, never imagining that these hulking brutes may soon arrive upon their doorstep.

ADVENTURE BACKGROUND

The inbred ogres of the Kreeg clanhold have long menaced the unfortunate or foolhardy folk who struggle to survive in the shadow of Hook Mountain. These ogres, more than any other clan dwelling upon the Hook, are aggressive, ravenous butchers, responsible for the slaughter of countless mining and lumber camps. Their raids are spurred by needs few sane minds can conceive of, driven by whatever brutish impulses their degenerate needs can muster.

Turtleback Ferry, a remote village not far from Hook Mountain, has long borne the brunt of Kreeg violence. Although closer to the city-state of Korvosa, it was Magnimar that answered the town's request for aid. Eager to extend their holdings and influence to the east, the lord-mayor of Magnimar established Fort Rannick to provide Turtleback Ferry with protection from the ogres, securing promises of regular taxes and trade. He stationed a band of rangers there—the Order of the Black Arrows—and charged them with keeping the region safe and free from ogres. The Kreegs were unprepared for any sort of organized defense by veteran rangers, and on their next raid they were met with efficient and swift punishment. The ogres retreated up to the heights of Hook Mountain and for many years made no major raids. Short but bloody skirmishes between the Kreegs and the Black Arrows have gone on for decades, but since their first decisive defeat at the entrance to the Valley of Broken Trees 45 years ago, the Kreegs have never quite built up enough bravery to mount a second attack on the well-defended Fort Rannick... until now.

A month ago, the Kreegs experienced a most unusual event—a visitor. Barl Breakbones was a boulder-bellied stone giant, a necromancer who towered a full five feet over the current Kreeg patriarch, Grolki. Sent by his master, Mokmurian, to subjugate the ogres of Hook Mountain and prepare their assimilation into the growing giant army, Barl's initial reception by the Kreegs was anything but friendly. When the ogres saw the fat giant approaching, they hooted, snarled, and spat before snatching up their rusty hooks, but Barl possessed powers beyond their ken. A necromancer who studied ancient magic from the secret ruins below the stone giant fortress of Jorgenhearth, Barl dispatched many of the ogres with ease (including their leader, Grolki), animating those he murdered as reinforcements against their kin. Grolki's son Jaagrath looked over the broken bodies of several of his favorite brother-sons and saw he had no choice—he raised a leathery hand to accept the opportunity to surrender.

Barl settled into his new role as chieftain of Hook Mountain with ease. Barl immediately set the Kreegs to work. They began forging massive weapons and shields from veins of iron, enough to arm the host of marauders gathering at the stone giant fortress of Jorgenharth.

The Order of the Black Arrows spotted plumes of greasy smoke rising from these forges and sent several scouts up the slopes to spy on the Kreegs. The rangers crept closer to the clanhold than ever before and observed the ogres toiling with their labors of iron and steel under the brutal hand of their enormous stone giant taskmaster. Alas, the ogres spotted the scouts when they tried to sneak closer, tearing them limb from limb, eager for a chance at vengeance against their hated enemies. Furious at the incursion and concerned the rangers might divulge his purpose, Barl decided to act against Fort Rannick.

Breakbones's plans were facilitated by another of his master's servants, a foul lamia matriarch known as Lucrecia, half-sister to the lamia matriarch Xanesha who recently troubled the city of Magnimar itself. Under orders from Mokmurian, Lucrecia arrived in Turtleback Ferry under the guise of an entrepreneur several years ago, when she bought an old barge and refurbished it as a floating gambling hall. She dubbed the barge *Paradise*, and offered any and all patrons myriad opportunities to enjoy themselves in her games of chance. *Paradise* was packed day and night with guests, and word of its decadent games and pleasures spread as far as Whistledown and Melfesh. Lucrecia used the den of sin as a place to foster and grow souls of greed to facilitate Karzoug's return. Favored guests were given small tattoos to show on following visits to receive discounts off the entrance fee and other, less seemly benefits. Of course, this tattoo was none other than the Sihedron Rune, and by so branding her customers, Lucrecia managed to prepare nearly half of Turtleback Ferry's populace for Karzoug's runewell.

Many were willing to be marked in order to enjoy *Paradise*'s "members-only" benefits, and even the steadfast Black Arrows of Fort Rannick weren't immune to the lure of love and easy money. One such unsteady soul, a skilled scout and archer named Kaven Windstrike, slipped out of the fort often to sate his desire for gold and women. Lucrecia recognized him by his gear and invited him into her parlor after telling him he'd won a special prize for being *Paradise*'s thousandth customer. There she charmed him and sent him back to Fort Rannick as her agent. Over the following months, Kaven's dependance on Lucrecia and the exotic offerings she provided only grew, to the extent that he is now firmly her minion even without magical control.

So when Barl Breakbones decided to mount a devastating raid on Fort Rannick, it was a simple matter for Lucrecia to organize several points of treachery to ensure the success of the coming assault. Lucrecia convinced Kaven to delay a large patrol of rangers returning from the wilds on the night of the raid, so that when the Kreegs descended on the fort they were able to breach the walls with minimal effort. A night of red ruin followed as the Kreegs added dozens of gore-slick skulls to their belts. They hooted as they feasted on the living men and women of the Black Arrows, and washed down their still-screaming heads with barrels of ale from the rangers' own stock. They danced their skull-jigs on the savaged bodies of their foes. They took turns torturing survivors, hanging them from trees on steel hooks to die slow horrible deaths twisting in the wind. Few rangers survived, and, including traitorous Kaven, they were quickly caught by a lesser family of ogrekin allied to the Kreegs—the horrifically inbred Grauls of Kreegwood.

Fort Rannick is now ruled by "Papa" Jaagrath Kreeg and his deformed family of deviants. Worried that her presence in

Turtleback Ferry was beginning to draw too much suspicion, Lucrecia abandoned *Paradise*, sinking it in Claybottom Lake while it was full of gamblers, and in so doing sending two dozen greedy souls to Karzoug. The lamia matriarch has relocated to captured Fort Rannick and now waits for the next stage in the plan—with the aid of a covey of hags manipulating the early winter storms, a flood is poised to destroy Turtleback Ferry. Already secretly marked with the Sihedron Rune, half the populace of the town are unknowingly set to fuel Karzoug's runewell when the ancient dam known as Skull's Crossing bursts.

Adventure Synopsis

After the PCs prove their mettle to the lord-mayor of Magnimar, he assigns them a dubious task: travel halfway across Varisia to check up on the town of Turtleback Ferry, the closest settlement to the strangely silent fort. Arriving in the town, the PCs find the place on edge, with stories of increasing ogre raids and worries on everyone's mind that something might have happened to Fort Rannick. Heading north, the PCs encounter a deformed ogrekin—a half-human, half-ogre menace—and after defeating him, they discover among his gear several items from Black Arrow rangers. The PCs can track this ogrekin back to his nearby home where they find the survivors of the raid on Fort Rannick kept by a family of inbred monsters—the Grauls.

After rescuing the rangers from the Grauls, the PCs learn about the massacre at Fort Rannick. Once they reach the fort, they must formulate a plan to retake it from the ferocious Kreeg ogres who now dwell within. After a grueling set of fights, the party retakes Fort Rannick only to suddenly find themselves in charge of the stronghold. Yet defeating the ogres at the fort does not end the region's problems.

Soon thereafter, unnatural rains flood Turtleback Ferry and the PCs must explore the ruins of an ancient dam called Skull's Crossing, repairing it enough so that its floodgates can be opened before the entire structure collapses. After saving the town from this disaster, the PCs learn that the ogres of Hook Mountain were to blame for the strange weather. After encountering the ghostly lover of the fort's previous (now dead) captain, the PCs finally climb Hook Mountain to end the ogre menace once and for all, only to learn that the ogres might be the least of Varisia's problems: the giants of the Storval Plateau are preparing for war.

PART ONE: IN THE HOOK'S SHADOW

Before you start "The Hook Mountain Massacre," give your PCs some time to recover from their ordeal with the Skinsaw Cult. They'll probably have treasure to spend, contacts to make, and magic items to craft—they might even wish to return to Sandpoint to visit with friends there or take care of outstanding business. This adventure begins in winter, so you should take some time here to impress upon the PCs the fact that the days are growing shorter and the rains are coming more and more frequently. Consult page 94 of the DMG for rules on how rain affects adventuring.

This adventure assumes that the PCs earned the favor of Magnimar's lord-mayor after revealing the Skinsaw Cult's plans for him. If the PCs haven't earned Lord-Mayor Grobaras's gratitude, though, they can still come to his attention when he hears reports of their actions in Sandpoint or their work in stopping the murders that have been plaguing both communities. New heroes like the PCs make perfect candidates for a problem that's just been brought to his attention—there's been no contact with Magnimar's most distant holding, remote Fort Rannick near Hook Mountain, for quite some time. The Black Arrows, the soldiers stationed at Fort Rannick, have traditionally been isolationists, but such a long silence is uncharacteristic even for them. Magnimar's Council of Ushers has been pressing Grobaras to send a patrol to Hook Mountain to investigate, but until the PCs came to his attention, Grobaras had no one he felt he could spare for what he viewed as a "pointless and silly trip to talk to those foul-tempered Black Arrows." Grobaras offers the PCs 300 gp each to cover their expenses for the trip and to pay them for their services—if the PCs ask for more, he grows flustered but can be talked up to 600 gp each with a DC 30 Diplomacy check.

How the PCs make the journey to Hook Mountain is left to them. You can spend as much or as little time on this journey as you wish, using the backdrop on Varisia that starts on page 60 to add details and wandering monster encounters to the trip as necessary. By land, it's a journey of 450 miles through lightly patrolled regions. By foot at a speed of 30 feet, this amounts to a 19-day journey, while on horseback at a speed of 60 feet it's only a 9-day trip. Alternatively, the PCs could take one of the many river barges that ply the Yondabakari and Skull Rivers from Magnimar all the way to Turtleback Ferry (at a total cost of 50 gp per person), in which case the journey takes only a week.

A Friendly Guide

As the PCs prepare for their journey, they are contacted by a familiar face—the elven ranger Shalelu Andosana. The PCs first encountered Shalelu during "Burnt Offerings," when she brought Sandpoint more news about the goblin threat. She might have joined with the group to face the goblins, or might even have developed a romantic relationship with one of the PCs. In any event, Shalelu's learned that the PCs are heading east to Fort Rannick, and she would like to accompany them on their journey. If she's in a relationship with one of the PCs, this alone is reason enough for her to tag along. Alternatively, if one of the PCs recently took Leadership, he might wish to recruit the elf as a cohort. Finally, the additional archery and survival support should be attractive to any group.

Of course, Shalelu's got her own reasons for wanting to make the journey to Fort Rannick. One of the rangers stationed there, a man named Jakardros, was at one time her mother's lover. Shalelu's memories of Jakardros are mostly of a young, exuberant man. She wasn't sure what her mother saw in the impulsive young human, but she was glad he was there for her. When her mother was slain in a dragon attack, Jakardros left suddenly and without explanation, leaving Shalelu with a bitter impression that eventually drove her into the isolated life she has lived for the past several years as a bounty hunter in the Sandpoint hinterlands. She recently learned that Jakardros has taken up with the Black Arrows of Fort Rannick and would very much like the opportunity to find out why the man abandoned her mother so abruptly after her death, if only to convince herself that he hadn't been taking advantage of her in some way. And if he had, Shalelu wants a chance to even the score.

SHALELU ANDOSANA   CR 5

Female elf ranger 3/fighter 2

CG Medium humanoid

Init +3; **Senses** low-light vision; Listen +9, Spot +3

DEFENSE

AC 17, touch 13, flat-footed 14

    (+4 armor, +3 Dex)

hp 38 (3d8+2d10+10)

Fort +7, **Ref** +6, **Will** +2; +2 against enchantment

Immune sleep

OFFENSE

Spd 30 ft.

Melee mwk short sword +7 (1d6+1/19–20)

Ranged +1 composite longbow +10 (1d8+2/×3) or

    +1 composite longbow +8/+8 (1d8+2/×3, Rapid Shot)

Special Attacks favored enemy +2 (goblinoid)

TACTICS

During Combat Shalelu prefers to fight with her bow, resorting to melee only when truly desperate or when an ally seems in dire need of healing from her wand.

Morale Shalelu is loyal to her friends, and as long as even one of them remains in danger she won't abandon them. If she feels she can escape, get help, and return in time to save anyone captured by enemies before it's too late, she might try.

STATISTICS

Str 12, **Dex** 16, **Con** 14, **Int** 10, **Wis** 13, **Cha** 8

Base Atk +5; **Grp** +6

Feats Dodge, Endurance, Point-Blank Shot, Precise Shot, Rapid Shot, Track, Weapon Focus (longbow)

Skills Climb +7, Hide +9, Listen +9, Move Silently +9, Search +2, Spot +3, Survival +7, Swim +7

Languages Common, Elven, Giant, Goblinoid

SQ wild empathy +2

Combat Gear wand of cure light wounds (34 charges); **Other Gear** +1 studded leather armor, +1 composite longbow (+1 Str) with 20 arrows, masterwork short sword, 125 gp

Hook Mountain Region

The area south of Hook Mountain is dominated by thick forests, lakes, and the swamps known as the Shimmerglens. While "The Hook Mountain Massacre" focuses on a few specific locations in this region, curious PCs could easily find more adventure here if they look.

Additional locations not mentioned here (such as Ashwood or Sanos Forest) are covered in the Varisia gazetteer that begins on page 60.

Bitter Hollow: Bitter Hollow is a filthy, remote thorp of about 50 hunters and trappers and their families. A single trading post called the Gator's Nest sits in the center of this settlement, and regular trade with the gnomes of the nearby Sanos Forest means that there are often unexpected items to purchase here.

Claybottom Lake: The fishing in Claybottom Lake is always good, but fishermen are quick to warn newcomers about the nightbelly boas, ravenous giant gars, and deadly giant snapping turtles that infest the lake's western reaches.

Kreegwood: Named for the ogres of Hook Mountain, although those who dwell in this woodland are mostly the half-human results of ogre lusts. The ogrekin that dwell here bicker among themselves, and rarely cause problems to outsiders. Anyone who ventures too far into these woods is fair game for dinner (or worse), though, so local villagers and hunters avoid this region entirely.

SHALELU
ANDOSANA

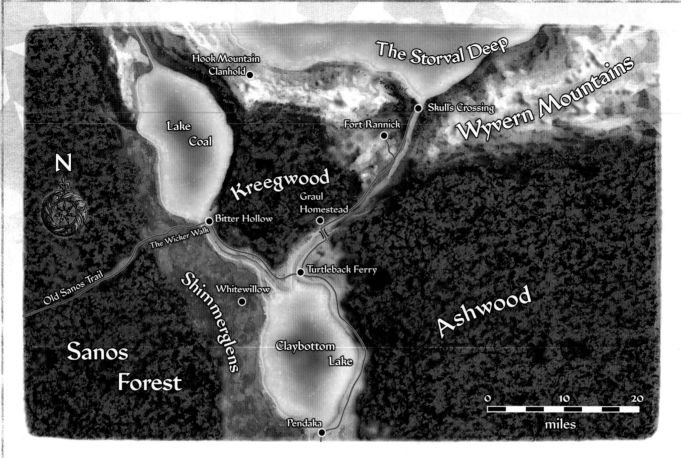

Lake Coal: The waters of Lake Coal are dark with silt and black algae. Fishing is poor in Lake Coal—not for the lack of fish, but for the ferocity of the large dark gars that dwell therein.

Old Sanos Trail: This narrow, claustrophobic forest trail winds deep into Sanos Forest, eventually connecting to several secluded gnome villages deep in the woods. Rumor holds that magic causes the trails to move when those who use them seek to bring trouble to the gnomes.

Pendaka: This tiny fishing thorp is perched on a rocky promontory overlooking the southern shores of Claybottom Lake. With its single combination inn/trading post, the Walleyed Wife, Pendaka's only claim to fame is local baker Olam Keecher's delicious cranberry turtle egg pies.

The Wicker Walk: Built by the founders of Bitter Hollow in a successful attempt to encourage trade with the gnomes of Sanos Forest, the Wicker Walk is a local marvel. The three-mile-long boardwalk is hung regularly with long-burning pitch lanterns, and its often-creaking boards offer the only completely dry path across the Shimmerglens.

Turtleback Ferry

Turtleback Ferry is a small township perched on the rain-drenched north shore of Claybottom Lake. Three distinctive ferries crafted from the shells of giant turtles slain by Autek Lavendy, one of the town's founders, make Turtleback Ferry the central trading town for the region. Nearly 80 miles from the next town of equitable size (Ilsurian), Turtleback Ferry has nominally been under Magnimarian

rule for 45 years, an arrangement the settlement agreed to in return for protection from the region's ogres and ogrekin.

Yet Turtleback Ferry remains independent in many ways, for its remote location ensures that official visits from Magnimar are few and far between. Turtleback Ferry's current mayor is an aged cleric of Erastil named Father Maelin Shreed, a selfless soul who tends to the village church as both a safe haven for travelers and a hospital wherein he tends the village's sick. Turtleback Ferry also boasts a trading post (The Turtleback General Store), an inn (The Turtle's Parlor), a tavern (Bottoms Up), and a smith (Irontooth's Metal Goods). Most of the village's other buildings are the homes of farmers, hunters, fishers, and trappers.

Visitors to Turtleback Ferry find the locals friendly enough, although many of them seem nervous and skittish, quick to lock their doors at night and often overreacting to the sound of dogs barking or other unexpected noises. This feeling is only partially due to the early arrival of the winter rains, and it shouldn't take long for the PCs to figure out that Magnimar's worries about Fort Rannick are anything but idle.

Questioning any of the villagers about the fort verifies that there's been no contact from the Black Arrows for several weeks now. Normally, one or two of the rangers visits Turtleback Ferry every few days for supplies, news, or entertainment, but since the rains began in earnest several weeks ago, no one's heard from the rangers at all. In addition, the wilds nearby (particularly Kreegwood) have grown more dangerous. Wild animals like bears, firepelt cougars, and boars are becoming increasingly common along the edges of these woodlands, and several of Turtleback's hunters and trappers believe these predators are being forced from the depths of the woodlands by the increased activity of local monsters like ogres, trolls, and worse. Earlier in the week, a patrol headed north to try to make contact with Fort Rannick, but they never returned.

TURTLEBACK FERRY

Village conventional (mayor); **AL** LN

GP Limit 200 gp; **Assets** 4,300 gp

DEMOGRAPHICS

Population 430

Type isolated (91% human, 5% gnome, 4% halfling)

AUTHORITY FIGURE

Maelin Shreed, mayor (LG male human cleric of Erastil 5)

Mark of the Sihedron

Every day the PCs spend in Turtleback Ferry, have them make DC 30 Spot checks. With a success, that PC notices a disturbing tattoo on one of the locals, hidden on the small of the back, the shoulder, or on the ankle. Exposed for a moment when the local bends over to pick up a crate or otherwise allows his clothing to slip, this tattoo is of a seven-pointed star—the same star the PCs have seen used by goblins and murderers over the past several weeks: the Sihedron Rune. If the tattooed local is confronted in a public place, he'll deny that he's got a tattoo while simultaneously attempting to make sure that his tattoo is covered up again. The villager's initial attitude to the PCs is unfriendly if confronted in this way, but if made friendly, he quietly admits that he got the tattoo a month ago at *Paradise*, a floating barge converted into a gambling and drinking hall that recently sunk. The villager sullenly explains that, by allowing *Paradise's* owner, the lovely and silken-tongued Lady Lucrecia, to place the tattoo on him for a small fee, he could then show the tattoo at *Paradise's* door and avoid paying the cover fee to board. Further, those who got "Paradise's Mark" (the Sihedron Rune) were often rewarded with additional gambling chits and other perks, and told that only a select few regular patrons had been chosen for the honor.

The villager admits he was coy about the tattoo because his wife would be furious if she found out he'd been spending enough time at *Paradise* to justify getting it, but defensively points out that he's not the only one in town with the mark. In fact, of Turtleback Ferry's population, 210 secretly bear the mark—far more than anyone in town suspects, since Lucrecia told them all to keep their tattoos a secret.

Investigations into the fate of Lady Lucrecia are destined to hit dead ends for now; everyone in town suspects she died in the fire that sank the barge several weeks ago. If the PCs wish to investigate the sunken barge, locals can point out the location on Claybottom Lake where the barge sank easily enough. The sunken barge lies under 60 feet of cold, dark water, and if located, all it reveals is a ruined wreck of a once fabulous floating den of sin. Lucrecia's already removed any evidence that the barge was anything but what the villagers thought it to be—but if the PCs insist upon exploring it, feel free to place a few monsters in its

ruins. An encounter with a school of six giant gars (use stats for Large sharks, MM 279) might make for a good encounter here, but if you use the *Tome of Horrors I* in your game, a more appropriate (and challenging) encounter would be one with a giant snapping turtle (page 266), one of the most dangerous predators in the lake.

It's certainly possible to remove a Sihedron Rune tattoo from a villager with an *erase* spell, but while doing so would rob Karzoug of the possibility of harvesting that villager's soul for his *runewell*, it won't stop Lucrecia's plans to destroy Turtleback Ferry by flooding it.

The Strange Bear (EL 8)

Eventually, the PCs should make their way north to Fort Rannick to see for themselves what's happened there. The simplest route is to follow an old road leading up along the banks of the Skull River. The road crosses an old wooden bridge to the western shore about three miles north of Turtleback Ferry, and from there heads all the way up to the impressive Thassilonian ruin known as Skull's Crossing, an immense stone dam that holds back the waters of the Storval Deep. A side road branches off about three miles before the dam, and a crooked wooden sign pointing up this trail proclaims "Fort Rannick."

Yet well before the PCs reach Fort Rannick, they run into something along the way. As they cross over the old wooden bridge near the location marked on the map as the Graul Homestead, have each PC make a Listen check. The PC that gets the highest result hears a muffled murmur of pain in the woods nearby, as if a large animal were wounded. If the PCs don't investigate at once, they soon hear barking dogs approaching from deeper in the woods, accompanied by a low voice singing an off-key song about eating bear. If the PCs still avoid investigating but remain behind to listen, the barking of the dogs soon grows excited, and the sound of combat between dogs, bear, and ogrekin becomes impossible to ignore.

If the PCs choose to ignore the sounds and continue north, let them. They'll reach Fort Rannick as detailed in Part Two, but without forewarning and aid from the surviving Black Arrow rangers kept at the Graul Homestead they might find themselves in over their heads.

Creatures: The wounded animal noise comes from Kibb, a black bear and the animal companion of Jakardros, one of the rangers who survived the ogre assault on Fort Rannick only to become the captive of a particularly foul and brutal band of ogrekin known as the Grauls. Kibb managed to escape and has spent the last three weeks eluding the Grauls (who've been desperately but poorly attempting to recapture the bear ever since) while trying to find someone whom he can lead back to the homestead to save his master. So far, none of the hunters Kibb has encountered realized that the bear was trying to get them to help, and now, the poor bear has fallen prey to one of their traps. His foot stuck in a bear trap, Kibb knows it's only a matter of time before the Grauls' best hunter, a lumbering half-ogre named Rukus, finds him and kills him.

Kibb grows excited if he sees human-sized creatures approaching, enough so that he advances, only to tug painfully at the iron bear trap around his back leg. A DC 15 Handle Animal, Knowledge (nature), or wild empathy check is enough to realize that the bear is well-trained and likely a druid or ranger's animal companion, while *speak with animals* allows a PC to learn the whole grim truth about what's going on (see Development, below). Kibb does not attack anyone who draws near unless they attack him first. A DC 28 Strength check (or a DC 20 Disable Device check) is enough to spring the trap and free the bear.

The sound of Rukus and his hounds broadcasts the ogrekin's arrival several rounds in advance, giving the PCs plenty of time to set up an ambush if they desire. The five hounds arrive first, howling and barking as they attempt to surround and attack Kibb or any other creatures they encounter. Rukus himself, a strapping young ogrekin with a wide mouth and one huge misshapen finger for a right hand barrels into the clearing 1d4 rounds later, gasping for breath after chasing the dogs for so long. Once he sees the PCs, he roars in anger: "I's huntin' bear! No concern o' you's less you's wanna be hunted too!"

RUKUS GRAUL   CR 7

Male ogrekin human fighter 6 (see page 90)

CE Medium giant

Init +5; **Senses** low-light vision; Listen +0, Spot +0

DEFENSE

AC 14, touch 11, flat-footed 13

  (+3 natural, +1 Dex)

hp 61 (6d10+24)

Fort +11, **Ref** +3, **Will** +2

OFFENSE

Spd 30 ft.

Melee +1 spear +13/+8 (1d8+13/×3)

TACTICS

During Combat Rukus sics his dogs on the PCs and watches the fight from the edge of the clearing for 1 round before he joins the fray. He prefers to fight against smaller or unarmored foes, flanking foes with his dogs when he gets the chance.

Morale Something of a coward, Rukus flees back to the Graul homestead if dropped below 30 hit points or if more than three of his dogs are slain, crying and blubbering loudly the entire way.

STATISTICS

Str 24, **Dex** 13, **Con** 18, **Int** 10, **Wis** 10, **Cha** 6

Base Atk +6; **Grp** +13

Feats Cleave, Improved Initiative, Great Fortitude, Power Attack, Skill Focus (survival), Track, Weapon Focus (spear), Weapon Specialization (spear)

Skills Handle Animal +7, Intimidate +11, Survival +7

Languages Common, Giant

SQ deformities

Gear +1 spear, belt of giant strength +2, favorite blanket (ratty, flea-infested, and decorated with several Black Arrow insignias)

SPECIAL ABILITIES

Rukus's Deformities (Ex) Rukus is particularly mean-looking and gains a +4 racial bonus on Intimidate checks. He cannot wield weapons with his deformed right hand and suffers a –2 penalty on attacks with two-handed weapons.

GRAUL HOUNDS (5)   CR 1

hp 13 each (MM 272; riding dog)

KIBB   CR 2

Black bear animal companion

hp 19 (currently 8; MM 269)

Development: If Rukus is taken alive, he barks savagely at the PCs when questioned. The ornery cuss refuses to give any information but his name unless his interrogators can shift his initial attitude of hostile to at least friendly, in which case Rukus launches into a long-winded, stuttering disclosure of his family's captives back at the "farmstead." Rukus likes patches and symbols a lot, and he brags about how "Mammy" sewed the insignias of dead captives to his favorite blanket—he proudly shows off the ratty, stained thing if asked, since he never leaves home without it tucked into the back of his belt. Five patches bearing the Black Arrow crest are sewn onto the blanket—in some cases, the patches are bloodstained. If Rukus is dead, the patches can be recognized for what they are with a DC 20 Knowledge (nobility and royalty) check. If Shalelu is with the party, she automatically recognizes the patches.

If Kibb survives, the bear frantically tries to communicate with the party. If they cannot *speak with animals*, a DC 20 wild empathy or Handle Animal check reveals that Kibb is very concerned about someone or something and wants the party to follow him. The bear nibbles at their cloaks, tugging them toward a poorly maintained trail that leads deeper into Kreegwood. If Rukus fled the battle, tracking him along the trail is a simple matter, and even if both Rukus and Kibb died in the battle, a DC 10 Search of the area reveals the partially overgrown path. Following it for a half mile leads to the Graul homestead.

The Graul Farm (EL 8 or 10)

This is where the PCs get their first taste of ogrish hillbilly horror. The Grauls are notorious in Kreegwood as one of the more disgusting and brave half-ogre families. Not only do these ogrekin have the grit to live less than half a mile from "man-land," but they do so with ease, snatching lone hunters and trappers with such quiet skill that they have yet to be discovered by the locals of Turtleback Ferry as the primary reason their woodsmen periodically go missing.

The Grauls dwell on a sickly farm in a clearing in the woods. The woods around their land are decorated with several hanging cornhusk-and-leather humanoid-shaped fetishes meant to ward off intruders—an investigation of any of these fetishes reveals they're stuffed with what appears to be a mix of dirt and human hair. A tangled field of corn and other diseased plants grows in the eastern section of their land, while to the north slump two sagging buildings: a barn and a farmhouse. Both have had their windows boarded over, and moss and fungus grow heavy on the shaded sides of the decrepit structures.

The Grauls are ruled by a notorious female known only as "Mammy" Graul, an accomplished cannibal, necrophile, and vile wizard. Grotesquely fat, Mammy Graul rarely moves beyond the walls of her reeking bedroom, letting her boys see to her needs—all of them. She's birthed dozens of strong ogrekin sons over the decades, and although her childbearing days are now behind her, she still enjoys visits from her sons and the occasional ogre from the highlands. She's long had an unhealthy crush on Jaagrath Kreeg, in fact, and when her boys caught several of the rangers who fled the massacre at Fort Rannick, she saw a chance to get herself further into the good graces of the powerful ogre. She's not sure how best to approach Jaagrath, though, and in the meantime has been running out of captives as they slowly succumb to the hungers and tortures of her sons. She's promised herself that she'll figure out what to do with them before they're all dead, but time is running short.

Creatures: While most of the Grauls prefer to spend their time indoors, either in the farmhouse or the barn, two of them prefer the outdoors. One of these two is Rukus, but if he survived his previous encounter with the PCs, he's already retreated to his room in the farmhouse (area **A6**) to nurse his wounds.

The second is an 8-foot-tall son Mammy Graul affectionately calls "Old Crowfood." Crowfood's grotesquely deformed head resembles a giant pumpkin on the right side—a huge puffy mass of tumors and overgrown bone giving his head a lopsided look. The ogrekin stalks the perimeter of the farmstead day and night, constantly on the lookout for intruders and working to scare crows and other animals away from his pride: the cornfield.

Crowfood automatically notices the PCs' approach unless they take pains to be stealthy. If he sees intruders, he gives cry and lumbers to attack. The sounds of battle here certainly alert the ogrekin within the buildings, but they prefer to wait inside for intruders to come to them rather than confront them out in the open—especially since their home is so riddled with cruel traps.

CROWFOOD   CR 8

Male ogrekin human rogue 4/fighter 3 (see page 90)
CE Medium giant
Init +1; **Senses** low-light vision; Listen +8, Spot +8

DEFENSE

AC 16, touch 12, flat-footed 15
(+1 deflection, +1 Dex, +4 natural)
hp 61 (4d6+3d10+28)
Fort +8, **Ref** +6, **Will** +5

Defensive Abilities evasion, trap sense +1, uncanny dodge

OFFENSE

Spd 30 ft.
Melee +1 ogre hook +14/+9 (1d12+10/×3)
Special Attacks sneak attack +2d6

TACTICS

During Combat Crowfood bellows and yells as he fights. Considerably braver than Rukus, he focuses his attacks on the largest foe, using a full Power Attack on the first round of combat (+8/+3 [1d12+22/×3]) and each round thereafter until he misses both attacks during a full attack, after which he gives up and makes normal attacks.
Morale Crowfood tries to flee into the barn (area **A16**) if brought below 15 hit points.

STATISTICS

Str 22, **Dex** 13, **Con** 18, **Int** 6, **Wis** 12, **Cha** 8
Base Atk +6; **Grp** +12
Feats Cleave, Dodge, Iron Will, Mobility, Power Attack, Weapon Focus (ogre hook)
Skills Climb +16, Escape Artist +8, Hide +8, Jump +13, Listen +8, Move Silently +10, Spot +8
Languages Giant
SQ deformities, trapfinding
Gear +1 ogre hook, ring of protection +1, amulet of natural armor +1, tattered rags and tunic

RUKUS GRAUL

SPECIAL ABILITIES

Crowfood's Deformities (Ex) Crowfood has a +2 racial bonus on Fortitude saves and heals damage twice as fast from rest. He's also quite ugly and suffers a −4 penalty on all Charisma-based checks.

A1. Farmhouse Porch (EL 5)

This giant decaying farmhouse covered in moss slumps drunkenly at the edge of the damp forest clearing. Rickety stairs crawl up to a porch covered by a huge eave held aloft by thick pillars of pine. These timbers are decorated with crude carvings of manticores impaling children with their tail spikes and women being ripped apart by wolves. The carvings look like a child's work, but the subject matter grows more gruesome and depraved from one depiction to the next. An unsettlingly large rocking chair of lashed wood and bone sways erratically in the breeze at the far end of the porch under a vast menagerie of wind chimes composed of decidedly humanoid bones. The house's windows have all been boarded up with thick timbers, although it's unclear if this was done to keep intruders out or imprison whatever unspeakable things make their home within.

A host of ants marches happily away here and there on the porch, many the size of a grown man's thumbnail. A moth the size of a shovel-head clings to the porch ceiling, watching the party with alien eyes, but it allows them to pass unmolested. The scent of bad meat, urine, sweat, and decay wafts now and then from between the cracks in the boarded-up windows, promising worse to any who seek to go inside.

Traps: Concealed cunningly among the hanging bone-chimes are a series of sharpened bone spurs mounted on a hinged rack rigged to swing down at anyone who touches the front door (the Grauls never use this entrance, preferring to come and go via the side door that opens into area **A4**). Additionally, several rusty saw blades are housed between the cracks of the porch's floorboards. When the door spikes are triggered, a series of crude pulleys and ropes under the porch creak to life, forcing the sawblades up between the cracks and slides them rapidly lengthwise, shearing through the feet of anyone standing in their way.

DOOR SPIKES   CR 3
Type mechanical
Search DC 20; **Disable Device** DC 25

EFFECTS

Trigger touch; **Reset** manual
Effect 4 bone spikes (+10 melee, 1d6 each)

FLOOR SAWS   CR 3
Type mechanical
Search DC 20; **Disable Device** DC 25

EFFECTS

Trigger location; **Reset** manual
Effect saw blades (+14 melee, 2d6+7); multiple targets (all creatures in area **A1**)

A2. Family Room (EL 3)

A mangy dire bearskin rug lies before a tremendous hearth set into the wall, its pained visage still snarling at whatever cruel hunter took its life. A huge couch haphazardly upholstered in animal hide and human flesh, replete with a collection of talons, monstrous hairy spider's legs, fox heads, and human hands and feet, sits to the west.

Trap: The western sofa is part of a hidden pit trap. Anyone coming within five feet of the sofa is in danger of falling through a hole in the floor into a chute lined with sharpened stakes coated in spider venom. The sofa itself is affixed to the wall via several sturdy timbers. It does not follow falling victims into area **A14** below.

PIT TRAP   CR 3
Type mechanical
Search DC 15; **Disable Device** DC 12

EFFECTS

Trigger location; **Reset** manual
Effect multiple targets (all characters adjacent to or on the sofa); fall (10 feet deep, Reflex DC 20 avoids); spikes (+15 melee, 1d4 spikes per target for 1d4+5 each plus poison), poison (spider venom, injury DC 14; 1d4 Str/1d4 Str)

A3. Dining Room (EL 3)

This dark room stinks of putrefying flesh. Eight wooden chairs with grinning bleached skulls crowning their backs circle a monstrous four-foot-high oak dining table covered with a crude tablecloth of crinkly human leather. The centerpiece of the dining table—a rotting human head, its stringy red hair thankfully draped over its mutilated face—serves as a gathering place for a host of buzzing, bloated flies.

Trap: Scythes attached to coils of tightly bound rope can be set to cut into anyone stepping through the doors to the west or east into this room. A hidden switch on the doors themselves allows the ogrekin to disable these traps before they come into the room, but if they hear combat outside, they make sure all three scythe traps are ready to go.

SCYTHE TRAPS (3)   CR 3
Type mechanical
Bypass hidden switch on each door (Search DC 20)
Search DC 25; **Disable Device** DC 25

EFFECTS

Trigger location; **Reset** manual
Effect large scythe (+15 melee, 2d6+4/×4)

A4. Kitchen

This musty chamber smells of week-old meat and is thick with clouds of fat, greasy flies. Thumb-sized cockroaches dance along the walls,

floor, and ceiling. A thick butcher's block sits under three cruel-looking cleavers hanging on a rack above. Bloodstained smocks of thick leather, one still dripping fresh gore, hang on bone-spur hooks by the door. A crockery platter of severed fingers and toes sits on a rickety old table next to a dried sinew basket overflowing with hacked-off hands and feet, all sporting stubs of congealed blood where their digits once were. A family of lucky rats gorges itself on the red stumps.

The smell in this room is horrific. Anyone (apart from one of the Grauls, who are all used to the stink) who enters this room must make a DC 15 Fortitude save to avoid becoming sickened for 1d6 minutes. The door to the north opens into a narrow stairwell that leads down into the basement.

Treasure: Despite their filthy condition, the three cleavers are exceedingly well-made and function as masterwork handaxes.

A5. Playpen (EL 5)

This simple room is strewn with "toys," some of carved wood or bone, while others appear to be little more than partial animal carcasses. Old bloodstains mark the walls, some in patterns that resemble crude child-like paintings featuring images of dismembered horses, a ridiculous grinning horned devil tossing children off a cliff, and a big lake with a black reptilian monster sprouting tentacles from its back. Bookshelves rest on the wall, but instead of tomes they hold skulls of all shapes and sizes.

Creatures: This playpen is where the two youngest Graul boys spend their time. Although both are full-grown, they act the most like spoiled children of all the Grauls, rarely emerging from this chamber into other parts of the farmhouse. Maulgro Graul is a hairless and pale bloated thing with malformed, stumpy legs and a wide mouth filled with ragged teeth. Maulgro keeps his skull collection here; he says he wants to be a Kreeg and someday dance the skull-jig when Mammy captures a priest-man to fix his dead legs. Mammy has no intention of doing so, as she finds the crippled boy's crawling amusing.

Maulgro's younger brother Lucky is here as well. Lucky's limbs bend in strange ways, but he's blessed to not have any other hideous deformity and almost looks human. Mammy doesn't like Lucky near as much as Maulgro and often neglects to even change the youngster's clothes for days at a time. The hapless fool reeks of his own waste as a result. He often steals Maulgro's favorite skulls to play keep-away, mocking the slower ogrekin to tears by dancing the skull-jig his brother will never dance himself.

LUCKY AND MAULGRO GRAUL   CR 3

hp 23 each (see page 90)

The Graul Homestead

Ground Floor

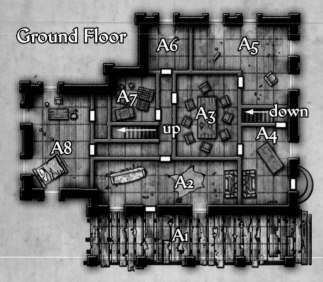

A6
A5
A7
A3
← down
A8
up
A4
A2
A1

Upper Floor

A9
←down→
A10

N

Basement

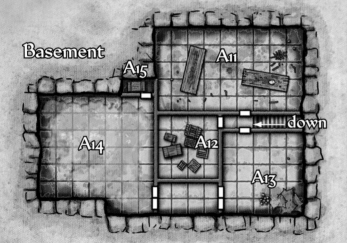

A15
A11
A14
A12
←down
A13

The Graul Farm

Barn

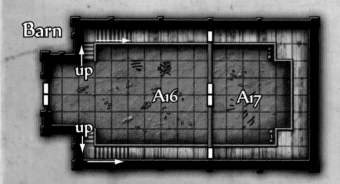

up
A16
A17
up

One Square = 5 Feet

One Square = 30 Feet

A6. Rukus's Room

This filthy bedroom contains little more than a lumpy mattress heaped with twigs, mud, and hopefully little else, although the stink of sewage in the room would seem to indicate otherwise. Dozens of vaguely humanoid fetishes crafted out of bits of leather, straw, corn husks, twigs, and bones hang from cords throughout the room.

This room belongs to Rukus—it's to here the cowardly ogrekin retreats a second time if he's attacked in the field outside the house. Cornered here, Rukus has little choice but to fight, and if he does so, he does so bravely, gaining a +2 morale bonus on attack rolls.

Treasure: Most of the fetishes hanging from the ceiling are worthless, but a DC 25 Search reveals that one of them incorporates several finger bones, one of which still wears a jade ring worth 300 gp.

A7. Privy

This closeted chamber is filled with stinking pits where the Grauls are expected to relieve themselves. One of the pits (the one closest to the west wall) is not used by the Graul boys. Instead this pit is filled with the tiny bones of every girl child Mammy has birthed—a grisly testament to the overabundance of men-folk in the Graul family. Mammy doesn't like female competition.

A8. Mammy's Room (EL 11)

The cloying stink of this room is nearly overwhelming. Buckets of filth are stacked against the walls, fat ravenous flies lazily circling their rims. The room itself is dominated by an immense bed, its ratty sheets stained beyond hope. A huge easel sits next to the bed with a palette of various shades of brown and red paint. The source of these morbid pigments—several crushed organs and ragged stumps of flesh—sit in receptacles next to the easel. A set of human-hair brushes jut from a broken skull by the easel, while a comb made from a human mandible sits on a small oak bedside table nearby, its teeth clotted with thick strands of greasy black hair. The bodies of three horribly deformed men dressed in ragged finery are propped up in huge open coffins against the far wall, their mouths sewn tightly shut with lengths of hair.

Creatures: This hellish room belongs to Mammy Graul, an incredibly corpulent monster with stringy hair and bald patches. Her obesity makes it difficult for her to move far, and she's been more or less confined to this reeking chamber for several years. She wears a huge red curtain as a shroud, and her bed creaks out in anguish as she shifts her massive form to regard any intruders to her home.

Mammy is also attended by three of her dead sons—Benk, Kunkel, and Hadge. Black Arrow rangers killed them all over the course of the last couple years, but Mammy "saved" them by casting *animate dead* on their remains, and now the three zombies serve her tirelessly. Benk has a useless third leg on his

left hip and a pin head—three arrows still protrude from his chest. Kunkel has an extra nose jutting from his right cheek and a hunched back, his head split by a ranger's axe. Hadge's deformities are hard to determine exactly. He was trampled to death by a charging warhorse and is now little more than a shambling fleshy bag of broken bones and mashed features that flops about when ordered to attack.

MAMMY GRAUL   **CR 9**

Female human ogrekin wizard (necromancer) 8

CE Medium giant

Init −3; **Senses** special senses; Listen +2, Spot +2

DEFENSE

AC 17, touch 7, flat-footed 17

  (+4 armor, −3 Dex, +6 natural)

hp 66 (8d4+32+13 from *false life*)

Fort +6, **Ref** −1, **Will** +6

OFFENSE

Spd 5 ft.

Melee mwk quarterstaff +10 (1d6+5)

Spells Prepared (CL 8th, +9 touch, +1 ranged touch)

  4th—*bestow curse* (DC 18), *contagion* (DC 18), *dimension door*

  3rd—*displacement*, *fly*, *summon monster III*, *vampiric touch*

  2nd—*blindness/deafness* (DC 16), *false life* (already cast), *ghoul touch* (DC 16), *mirror image*, *summon monster II*

  1st—*chill touch* (DC 15), *grease* (DC 13), *mage armor* (already cast), *ray of enfeeblement*, *reduce person* (DC 13), *true strike*

  0—*mage hand* (3), *message*, *touch of fatigue* (DC 14)

Prohibited Schools abjuration, enchantment

TACTICS

Before Combat As soon as she hears trouble outside, Mammy Graul casts *mage armor* and *false life* on herself. If she realizes someone's about to enter her room, she casts *mirror image* and *fly* as well.

During Combat If the PCs confront Mammy Graul here, she's more enraged at her boys for allowing the PCs to get this far than she is at the PCs themselves, and her profanity-laced shrieks against her boys fill any surviving Grauls with such fear that none of them dare come to their mother's aid. Mammy Graul sends her three zombies to engage the PCs while she remains on her bed in the northwest corner of the room and casts spells. She starts with *summon monster* spells and follows up with her ranged spells. Once anyone reaches her in melee, her first act is to cast *mirror image* (if she hasn't already), and then cast her melee spells.

Morale If reduced to 20 hit points or less, she attempts to *dimension door* into area **A16** to secure the aid of any surviving Grauls there. She casts *fly* on herself and leads them back to the farmhouse to attack the PCs again, this time fighting to the death.

STATISTICS

Str 20, **Dex** 4, **Con** 19, **Int** 15, **Wis** 10, **Cha** 10

Base Atk +4; **Grp** +9

Feats Alertness (when Blub-Blug is in arm's reach), Brew Potion, Craft Wand, Craft Wondrous Item, Greater Spell Focus (necromancy), Scribe Scroll, Spell Focus (necromancy)

Skills Concentration +15, Knowledge (arcana) +13, Spellcraft +15

Languages Abyssal, Common, Giant

SQ deformities, summon familiar (toad named Blub-Blug)

Combat Gear potion of cure moderate wounds, scroll of animate dead, wand of magic missile (CL 3rd, 44 charges), wand of ray of enfeeblement (28 charges), wand of vampiric touch (33 charges); **Other Gear** amulet of health +2, Varisian idols (2, grant summoned monsters +2 hp per HD if used as an additional material component—see the Rise of the Runelords Player's Guide)

SPECIAL ABILITIES

Mammy's Deformities (Ex) Mammy Graul's thick layers of blubber increase her natural armor bonus by an additional 3 points. She is also hideously overweight, and suffers a −4 penalty to her Dexterity.

BLUB-BLUG   CR —
Toad familiar

hp 26 (MM 282)

BENK, KUNKEL, AND HADGE   CR 1/2
Ogrekin zombies

hp 55 each (MM 267; use human zombies)

A9. Bedroom (EL 3)

This room is filled with large, filthy beds. Human skulls with antlers fixed to them are mounted on the bedposts and headboards. Against the west wall sits a large cedar chest.

This is where most of the Graul boys sleep when they aren't bedding down in the barn.

Trap: The chest in this room is one of the boys' favorite toys. Although not locked, the chest's lid sticks and must be wrenched open with a DC 20 Strength check. Opening the chest triggers no traps and reveals a sack of coins within. Unfortunately, the coins sit on a pressure trigger set to release a cleverly concealed war razor housed within the wall of the chest. As soon as the sack is lifted, this blade snaps out with tremendous force. The blade is also laced with poison. The boys enjoy daring each other to "beat the blade," but not quite as much as telling prisoners that they'll be let free if they can get the chest open and steal the coins.

HAND CHOPPER   CR 3
Type mechanical

Search DC 20; **Disable Device** DC 25

EFFECTS

Trigger touch; **Reset** manual

Effect war razor (+12 melee, 1d4+8/18–20 plus poison); poison (spider venom, injury DC 14; 1d4 Str/1d4 Str)

Treasure: The sack of coins contains a mix of 121 cp, 110 sp, and 23 gp, along with seventeen mostly skeletal severed fingers—trophies from the hand chopper trap collected and stored here by the ogres.

A10. Attic

Tables strewn with beakers, glass vials, old tin cans, rope, animal traps, bits of twisted metal, spikes, bones, and all manner of junk litter this area. In one corner sits some old furniture and other keepsakes.

This area is the workshop of Hucker Graul; the eldest of Mammy's boys and the mastermind behind the devious traps that lace this building. Hucker himself lives in a room in the basement (area **A12**).

Treasure: Five flasks of acid are stored under one of the tables. With 1d10 minutes of scrounging, three full sets of masterwork thieves' tools can be scavenged from the gear here.

A11. Skin Shucking Room

This dark, recessed corner of the basement smells of rot and old blood. Piles of gore-spattered skin lie heaped on the floor. A horrid rubbery face robbed of its supporting skull and muscle rests on top, its toothless mouth agape and empty eyes revealing only the layer of tan flayed skin resting beneath.

Much of the furniture in the farmhouse above is upholstered in human leather or decorated with human bones. This grim room is where Hucker Graul prepares skins and bones for just such purposes. The face on the pile of skin once belonged to one of the Black Arrow rangers—Hucker hasn't decided what to do with it yet.

A12. Hucker's Lair (EL 8)

This low-ceilinged room features a floor of hard-packed earth stained in many places by blood and mold. A lumpy mattress lies heaped against the southwest corner, and what appear to be several half-finished chairs made of flesh and bone lie against the eastern wall.

Creatures: Hucker Graul creeps around here in the dark below the farmhouse. As the eldest of Mammy's sons, Hucker is also the most responsible of the Grauls. His gift for trapmaking and knack for building furniture keeps the farmhouse defended and relatively comfortable. He has little patience for his brother-sons, though, and if he hears traps sprung above or the sounds of combat, he makes a note that he'll need to reset the traps later but doesn't come investigate, assuming the other Grauls are simply having another of their petty disagreements or are tormenting a new prisoner.

Hucker shuffles with a pronounced limp from an old injury suffered when one of his own traps backfired on him, a wound he bears with misplaced pride. Hair grows lopsided from the right side of his head and face rather than atop his brow, and a vestigial twin capable of grunting and gasping protrudes from the back of his neck. Hucker's best friends are two overgrown donkey rats he named Chuckles and Drooler. They eagerly defend their master, chewing intruders to pieces.

HUCKER GRAUL   CR 8

Male ogrekin human barbarian 1/rogue 5

CE Medium giant

Init +7; **Senses** low-light vision; Listen +10, Spot +1

DEFENSE

AC 20, touch 11, flat-footed 17

(+5 armor, +3 Dex, +4 natural, −2 rage)

hp 59 (1d12+5d6+30)

Fort +8, **Ref** +7, **Will** +6

Defensive Abilities evasion, trap sense +1, uncanny dodge; **Immune** charm effects

OFFENSE

Spd 40 ft.

Melee +1 ogre hook +13 (1d12+12/×3)

Special Attacks rage 1/day, sneak attack +3d6

TACTICS

During Combat Hucker rages on the first round of combat and sends his rats to attack the PCs while he delays so he can move into a flanking position once the rats go.

Morale If brought below 25 hit points, Hucker attempts to retreat to area A14, hoping to lure the PCs into a fight with the tendriculos the Grauls keep there. He then fights to the death.

Base Statistics When not raging, Hucker's stats change as follows:

AC 22, touch 13, flat-footed 19

hp 47

Fort +6, Will +4

Melee +1 ogre hook +11 (1d12+8/×3)

Str 20, Con 16

Skills Climb +10, Jump +18

STATISTICS

Str 24, **Dex** 16, **Con** 20, **Int** 6, **Wis** 13, **Cha** 8

Base Atk +4; **Grp** +11

Feats Improved Initiative, Power Attack, Skill Focus (Craft [trapmaking]), Weapon Focus (ogre hook)

Skills Climb +8, Craft (trapmaking) +10, Handle Animal +3, Hide +8, Jump +20, Listen +10, Move Silently +8, Use Rope +8

Languages Giant

SQ deformities, trapfinding

Combat Gear potion of cure moderate wounds; **Other Gear** +1 hide shirt, +1 ogre hook, amulet of natural armor +1, collection of severed noses in wax-sealed tin

SPECIAL ABILITIES

Hucker's Deformities (Ex) Hucker has a deformed vestigial twin growing from the back of his neck, granting him a +2 racial bonus on Will saves. His malformed jaw gives him a speech impediment and a −2 penalty on any skill check that relies on speech.

CHUCKLES AND DROOLER   CR 3

Advanced donkey rats (variant dire rat)

N Medium animal

Init +3; **Senses** low-light vision, scent; Listen +6, Spot +3

DEFENSE

AC 14, touch 13, flat-footed 11

(+3 Dex, +1 natural)

hp 33 (6d8+12)

Fort +7, **Ref** +8, **Will** +6

OFFENSE

Spd 40 ft., climb 20 ft.

Melee bite +7 (1d8+3)

TACTICS

During Combat Both donkey rats focus their attacks on the same target each round, preferring smaller foes over larger ones.

Morale A donkey rat flees if brought below 5 hit points.

STATISTICS

Str 14, **Dex** 16, **Con** 14, **Int** 1, **Wis** 12, **Cha** 4

Base Atk +4; **Grp** +6

Feats Alertness, Combat Reflexes, Improved Natural Attack, Weapon Finesse

Skills Climb +11, Hide +8, Listen +6, Move Silently +8, Spot +3

MAMMY GRAUL

A13. Storeroom

It's difficult to gauge the exact dimensions of this cluttered room, so thickly packed with old crates, broken farm equipment, and furniture as it is.

Most of the things the Grauls break eventually end up stacked in this room. Hucker periodically sifts through the junk for raw materials for his projects, but currently there's little of value in here.

A14. Tendriculos Pit (CR 6)

This damp, steamy room reeks of rotting vegetable matter. Pools of mud and stagnant water dot the mossy floor, and the walls are caked with thick swaths of puffy fungus and mold.

Creature: This mossy, vine-covered section of the basement is home to one of the least fortunate of the Grauls. Ironically, Muck Graul used to be one of the handsomest of Mammy's boys, but after he caught and tortured a nymph princess for days on end, she spat a foul curse upon him with her dying breath. Muck began a slow, painful transformation, his flesh showing strange greenish sores and moss growing from his orifices. His limbs grew spongy and insubstantial until he collapsed into a shuddering mass of plant matter. Mammy consigned him to the basement to keep him from "mussing up the house." Muck grew day after day, nurtured by his brothers even as they ridiculed him for his new hideous appearance. Muck Graul is now a massive tendriculos. He barely remembers his life before, and although he recognizes the Grauls as allies, he attacks anyone else who enters this room.

MUCK GRAUL   **CR 6**

Tendriculos

hp 94 (MM 241)

A15. The Graul Fortune

A single large chest sits against the wall of this low-ceilinged chamber.

Treasure: While the Grauls have used most of the loot taken from their victims over the years to pay tribute to the Kreegs, they've kept hold of a fair amount of treasure for themselves. This loot is kept here, in this unlocked chest. Within lies an agate-studded gold ring worth 50 gp, a necklace of emeralds and silver worth 350 gp, a pair of small leather gloves studded with pearls (actually *gloves of Dexterity +2*), a large sack filled with assorted coins (210 gp, 452 sp, and 108 cp), a ruby-inlaid red dragon-scale cloak clasp worth 600 gp, and an elven-made *+1 shocking longbow*. If Shalelu is with the party, her eyes widen at this weapon—it belongs to Jakardros, her stepfather. If she's already revealed her relationship with the ranger, she'll reveal the bow's owner to the PCs at this time; otherwise she remains silent for now and hopes the weapon's presence here doesn't indicate that Jakardros is already dead.

A16. Kennel (EL 7)

The barn houses several mounds of molding hay, grain stores, and even a large but crude still. Two catwalks rise up along the walls, leading to doors near the ceiling in the east wall. Lower, a pair of massive doors, boarded over with thick timbers, allow ground access to the room beyond. Several dingy kennels are built into the walls under the catwalks.

If any of Rukus's hounds survived the initial encounter with the PCs, they've been kenneled here. The boarded-up door to area **A17** is clogged on the far side by thick webs. Wrenching it open is nearly impossible and requires a DC 36 Strength check.

The still functions, but the moonshine it produces is foul and nauseating—the Graul boys have never cleaned the thing, and the ingredients they use to brew the stuff are suspect at best. A character who drinks from the still must make a DC 14 Fortitude save to avoid being nauseated for 1d6 rounds and must make a second DC 16 Fortitude save to avoid catching blinding sickness (DMG 292) from the contaminated booze.

Several keys hang on a bent nail by the main entrance; these keys are for the manacles in the cages in area **A17**.

Creatures: Three of the younger Grauls (Jeppo, Hograth, and Sugar) spend most of their time here, drinking away their days and periodically inflicting unimaginable tortures on any captives kept in area **A17**.

Hograth is the eldest of these three, a hulking brute with a vestigial arm growing from his left elbow and a no-necked dented head. Jeppo Graul is a big, handsome boy towering over his brothers. His eyes are huge and milky white, and his skin pale as the full moon. Sugar is the shortest of the Grauls, standing barely more than five feet tall, with crooked stumpy legs and constantly twitching skin.

These Graul boys take their charge of tending to the Black Arrow prisoners in area **A17** very seriously and ignore any sounds of combat elsewhere on the property unless Mammy Graul flees here to recruit their aid in mounting an assault on the PCs.

HOGRATH, JEPPO, AND SUGAR GRAUL   **CR 3**

hp 23 each (see page 90)

SPECIAL ABILITIES

Hograth's Deformities (Ex) Hograth has a vestigial arm that grants him a +4 racial bonus on grapple checks, but has a deformed head (and corresponding weak mind) that imparts a –2 penalty on Will saves.

Jeppo's Deformities (Ex) Jeppo's overlarge, milky eyes grant him a +2 bonus on Search and Spot checks but are also sensitive to light (exposure to bright light dazzles him for as long as he remains in the area).

Sugar's Deformities (Ex) Sugar is particularly jumpy—a manifestation of a fast metabolism that grants him a +2 racial bonus on Fortitude saves and doubles his healing from rest, but his stunted legs reduce his speed to 20 feet.

A17. Prison (EL 7)

The majority of this large, stuffy chamber is covered in filthy webs forming a funnel that dips down into the ground. A catwalk runs around the rim of the room near the ceiling, twenty feet above the ground. In each corner, the catwalk expands into a ten-foot-square platform that's fenced in by wooden beams, forming a cage in each corner. The walls within each cage are hung with iron manacles. Most of the manacles—while bloody—are empty, but three in the southeast corner imprison emaciated men.

Anyone who falls into the thick webs below takes no falling damage but does immediately become entangled in the webs of the Huge spider that dwells below (MM 289).

Creatures: One of the Grauls' pride and joys, the immense funnel-web spider that dwells in this room is also one of their least-behaved pets. The Grauls call the spider "Biggin'," and most of them have been bitten by the monstrous spider before. Still, the spider's too mindless to bother trying to get to anything locked in the two cages in the upper corners of the room. As long as the Grauls keep the thing fairly well-fed, and make sure to throw a deer, pig, gnome, or other sizable animal into the web before they venture in to check the cages, Biggin' leaves those moving around on the catwalk alone.

Of course, the PCs aren't likely to know this. The immense spider scurries up out of its web to attack if no offering of food has been thrown into its web within four rounds of someone entering this room.

All three of the humans locked in the southeast cage are unconscious—they are the last three surviving Black Arrow rangers from Fort Rannick.

BIGGIN' · CR 7

Advanced elite monstrous funnel-web spider (MM 289)

N Huge vermin

Init +4; **Senses** darkvision 60 ft., tremorsense 60 ft.; Listen +1, Spot +5

DEFENSE

AC 17, touch 12, flat-footed 13

(+4 Dex, +5 natural, −2 size)

hp 133 (14d8+70)

Fort +14, **Ref** +8, **Will** +5

Immune mind-affecting effects

OFFENSE

Spd 30 ft., climb 20 ft.

Melee bite +14 (2d6+9 plus poison)

Space 15 ft.; **Reach** 10 ft.

Special Attack poison (DC 22, 1d8 Str/1d8 Str), web

TACTICS

During Combat Once Biggin' scuttles forth from its nest deep in the webs below, it has little problem clambering up the sides of its web to attack anything on the ledges above. It won't attack anyone in the caged areas unless a target it already pursues seeks shelter in a cage, at which point the monster tears that cage apart to get at anything inside.

Morale Biggin' fights to the death.

STATISTICS

Str 22, **Dex** 19, **Con** 20, **Int** —, **Wis** 12, **Cha** 2

Base Atk +10; **Grp** +24

Skills Climb +14, Hide +0 (+8 in webs), Move Silently +4 (+12 in webs), Spot +5

Last of the Black Arrows

The Order of Black Arrows has been a secretive and insular order for decades, since its founding by Zarnath Rannick. Traditionally a wandering order of hunters and rangers dedicated to patrolling the Storval Rise, the Black Arrows saw it as their duty to prevent giant incursions from the plateau into Varisia. When Magnimar offered the order a fort in the shadow of Hook Mountain, Zarnath accepted graciously but died in a battle against the Kreeg ogres before the fort was completed. His men named the keep after him, and ever since, Fort Rannick has been instrumental in keeping the ogres, trolls, and other giants of the region from spreading too far into the lowlands.

During the 45 years they've been stationed at the fort, the Black Arrows inducted new members often—typically petty criminals given a choice between severe punishment or a lifetime sworn to manning the walls of the fort and patrolling the perilous heights of Hook Mountain. Conditions at Fort Rannick swiftly made honest men out of most of these criminals, forcing them to engage in a vicious regimen of training that stripped away all sense of their life prior to joining the order. The task of keeping the horrors of the Hook at bay is a grueling one and requires a level of discipline unattainable by many soldiers. They have a reputation for dealing with trouble among the ranks of the order in their own way—coldly and efficiently. Those who disobey commands are flogged near to death before being exiled to the south. Those who betray the order are mercilessly executed. Their justice swift, their reputation fierce, it wasn't until three weeks ago that the Black Arrows finally met their match—and then only due to treachery from within.

Of the dozens who once comprised the Order of the Black Arrow, only three survive today, and they are in bad shape. The only reason this group escaped the slaughter at the fort was because they were on a long-range patrol during the massacre. Their leader, a weathered old ranger whose worn face is as hard as leather, is named Jakardros. He and two of his men (Kaven and Vale) are all that remain; the other men in the patrol have already been taken away for torture and death at the Grauls' hands.

All three men are currently unconscious and at 0 hit points.

Jakardros Sovark

Jakardros lost his eye to a close call with an ogre hook a decade ago. For many years second-in-command of Fort Rannick under Captain Bayden, Jakardros saw his commander carried off by the ogres just as his patrol arrived at Fort Rannick—too late to aid in its defense. He lost a third of his men in an attempt to retake the fort, and when they were forced to flee south into Kreegwood, the remaining men were easy targets for the Grauls. Jakardros carries the loss of Fort Rannick heavily and feels it was his fault that the ogres were able to take it. Had he been a bit more prompt on his patrol, he would have been back in time to help defend the place. But he wasn't, and now a 45-year tradition is dead.

When Jakardros was younger and before he joined the Black Arrows, he spent a few years as an adventurer. His group eventually ended up in the region around the Mierani Forest, where they helped a small village of elves defeat a group of murderous ettercaps led by a green dragon. Jakardros's adventuring companions all perished in the fight, giving their lives for the elven community of Crying Leaf. Jakardros was nursed back to health by an elven priestess of Desna there, and the two of them fell in love. Jakardros would have lived the rest of his life in Crying Leaf had not his lover, Seanthia, herself perished when the village was attacked by the resurrected dragon three years later. With Jakardros's aid, the town defeated the dragon again, but Jakardros was too broken-hearted to remain. He gathered his belongings and, within minutes of the dragon's death, left Crying Leaf behind him, along with the sorrowful task of attending to Seanthia's funeral. His heart hardened, he eventually heard of the Black Arrows and applied for membership, hoping that service to the order would help him bury his broken heart.

To a certain extent, his plan worked. But now that Fort Rannick is lost, his old melancholy has returned—the loss of the fort wakening similar memories of Seanthia's death. He bitterly regrets abandoning Crying Leaf, and between wishing he'd died in either the second dragon attack or in the more recent ogre attack, his mood has grown increasingly dark, almost suicidal.

And unfortunately for Jakardros, his life is about to grow even more complex, for his stepdaughter is none other than Shalelu Andosana.

JAKARDROS SOVARK   CR 8

Male middle-aged human ranger 8
CG Medium humanoid
Init +2; **Senses** Listen +11, Spot +11

DEFENSE

AC 12, touch 12, flat-footed 10
  (+2 Dex)
hp 55 (currently 0; 8d8+16)
Fort +8, **Ref** +8, **Will** +4

OFFENSE

Spd 30 ft.
Melee unarmed strike +8 (1d3 nonlethal)
Special Attacks favored enemies (dragon +2, giant +4)
Spells Prepared (CL 4th)
  2nd—*cure light wounds* (already cast)
  1st—*animal messenger* (already cast), *speak with animals* (already cast)

TACTICS

During Combat Jakardros's strengths are in archery, with a strong preference toward fighting from horseback. He trusts (and depends) on his men and his animal companion Kibb to hold off

foes in melee while he provides ranged support. Yet when his allies are in desperate need, he won't hesitate to lay down his bow and join them in melee.

Morale Jakardros has little concern for his own safety, and is actively looking for a foe that can finish him off. He fights to the death as a result. Once he's reconciled with Shalelu, though, his outlook shifts dramatically; he devotes his life to protecting the elven ranger, doting on her as if she were his own daughter. He'll fight to the death to protect her, but otherwise breaks off combat and retreats if brought below 20 hit points so he can stay alive to defend Shalelu in the future.

STATISTICS

Str 11, **Dex** 15, **Con** 14, **Int** 11, **Wis** 14, **Cha** 9
Base Atk +8; **Grp** +8
Feats Endurance, Manyshot, Mounted Archery, Mounted Combat, Point Blank Shot, Precise Shot, Rapid Shot, Track
Skills Handle Animal +10, Hide +13, Listen +13, Move Silently +13, Ride +15, Spot +13, Survival +13
Languages Common, Giant
SQ animal companion (black bear named Kibb), swift tracker, wild empathy +9, woodland stride

Vale Temros

Vale is a dark-skinned man with piercing gray eyes. At a towering height of 6–1/2 feet, his build and musculature consigned him to the warrior's path at an early age. Despite his stature, Vale is a quiet and withdrawn man whose passion for life only wakens during the heat of battle.

Vale was born into the Order of the Black Arrow; both his parents were members, as were his two younger brothers. All of them are now dead, slain either years ago (in the case of his parents) or weeks ago (in the case of his brothers) by various Kreeg ogres. Vale's oath of vengeance against the Kreegs has become the only thing holding him together over the past several days of torture and mind-numbing horror at the Grauls' hands. Given the chance to strike back at the ogres, Vale siezes the opportunity with grim satisfaction.

Apart from his prowess in battle, Vale also had a passing fancy for sieges and architecture, and spent many of his off hours in the fort talking with the resident architect, a now-dead man named Drannis. Apart from battle, discussions about normally dry and boring topics like engineering and buildings are among the few times that Vale breaks out of his taciturn shell to become excited and animated.

VALE TEMROS   CR 6

Male human ranger 2/fighter 4
NG Medium humanoid
Init +1; **Senses** Listen +1, Spot +6

AN AWKWARD REUNION

If Shalelu is with the PCs when they rescue the Black Arrows, her reunion with Jakardros is awkward and strange, especially if she hasn't revealed to the PCs that the man was her mother's lover. Shalelu confronts him silently, and after a few moments, Jakardros recognizes her. In the decades since last they met, she hasn't aged a day, whereas he's become a grizzled old man. In her, he sees the specter of her mother, and he breaks down into a fit of sobs that greatly unnerves Vale and amuses Kaven. It's certainly not the reaction Shalelu expected. In the days to come, Jakardros begins to see a chance at salvation in Shalelu, and grows more and more into the role of protective father, a role that might put him at odds with one of the PCs if he's become Shalelu's lover. Shalelu quickly warms to Jakardros, in any event, and when not aiding the PCs in retaking the fort, the two spend the hours recounting stories about her mother and catching up on old times.

DEFENSE

AC 11, touch 11, flat-footed 10
   (+1 Dex)
hp 46 (currently 0; 2d8+4d10+12)
Fort +9, **Ref** +5, **Will** +2

OFFENSE

Spd 30 ft.
Melee unarmed strike +9 (1d3+3 nonlethal)
Special Attacks favored enemy (giants +2)

TACTICS

During Combat Although Vale pays little attention to how much damage he takes during a fight, he certainly doesn't fight recklessly. He approaches battle with a wide-eyed excitement, viewing each fight as a puzzle to be solved with mind and steel. He has a knack for seeking out subtle tactical advantages (higher ground, flanking, cover, and the like) that serve him well. Vale prefers to fight with a battleaxe and handaxe, and once an enemy is engaged, he makes increasing Power Attacks until he can't quite hit foes with his secondary attacks. He views his greatest flaw as his lack of particular talent in finesse fighting, and when he grows too overconfident, he often makes trip, disarm, and flanking attacks that provoke a dangerous number of attacks of opportunity.

Morale Left on his own, the concept of retreat would never occur to Vale. He becomes so enthralled with the battle that he loses track of his own well-being.

STATISTICS

Str 16, **Dex** 13, **Con** 14, **Int** 10, **Wis** 12, **Cha** 8
Base Atk +6; **Grp** +9
Feats Cleave, Great Fortitude, Power Attack, Track, Two-Weapon Fighting, Weapon Focus (battleaxe, handaxe), Weapon Specialization (battleaxe, handaxe)
Skills Climb +9, Craft (stonemason) +9, Knowledge (architecture and engineering) +4, Profession (siege engineer) +5, Search +5, Spot +6, Survival +6
Languages Common, Giant, Sylvan
SQ wild empathy +0

VALE
TEMROS

Kaven Windstrike

Kaven Windstrike, a handsome young man with dark hair and emerald eyes, has traditionally been able to get what he wants out of life via his good looks and smooth tongue. A wayward youth born to harried parents in Turtleback Ferry, Kaven's antics finally got him in over his head when he assaulted and robbed an old goatherd who turned out to be a long-time family friend. Infuriated, his father was all but ready to press charges and have the boy taken south by the law to serve time in a jail in Ilsurian, but his mother managed to temper that reaction. Kaven was was given a choice: be disowned and spend time in prison, or seek membership among the Black Arrows. His father always admired the order, and figured if they couldn't shape Kaven into an upstanding man, no one could. Kaven, balking at the thought of prison, chose the Black Arrows.

At first, the disciplined lifestyle did Kaven good, and he reformed into a respected and effective member of the order. However, when Lady Lucrecia opened *Paradise's* gambling halls to the public a year ago, Kaven and two other Black Arrows snuck down to the barge one night to sample its offerings. It was enough to remind Kaven what he liked about the quick and exciting life of gambling, high risk, and crime. Kaven volunteered for the weekly southern patrol (a route most of the Black Arrows disliked due to its relatively boring route along the eastern shore of Claybottom Lake). Rather than spending his nights in Turtleback Ferry or Pendakus, though, he took to spending them at *Paradise*. Of course, Lucrecia recognized him as one of the Black Arrows and, knowing that having an ally on the inside might someday be a vital boon, she seduced him, charmed him, and made him her pet.

As the months wore on, Kaven fell deeper and deeper into Lucrecia's thrall, to an extent that she no longer needed to keep him charmed. He not only began to steal from his fellow rangers to fund his secret nights of debauchery in *Paradise*, but in the end it was he who betrayed them at Lady Lucrecia's request. Kaven gave her all the information about patrols and defenses she needed to ensure a swift and decisive strike on Fort Rannick, and then Kaven volunteered for the patrol that would keep him out of the fort when the assault came. He even engineered several delays during that patrol to ensure they would not return to the fort in time to provide aid in the fight. What Kaven hadn't counted on was being captured by the Grauls—Lucrecia had promised to flee the region with him once the attack was over, and he had planned on meeting her at a prearranged time in Turtleback Ferry. In fact, Lucrecia planned to murder him at that meeting, so even though he doesn't realize it, being captured by the Grauls actually saved his miserable life.

For the past several days, Kaven has feigned loyalty to the dwindling number of Black Arrows, caught between the horror of being found out by his brothers and the possibility of being the next one chosen for torture and dinner by the Grauls. When the PCs rescue the Black Arrows, Kaven pretends at helpfulness during preparation for the assault on Rannick but secretly keeps an eye out for a chance to finish his betrayal and escape to Turtleback Ferry so he can track down his lover, unaware of the fact that she's already written him off as ogrekin food.

KAVEN WINDSTRIKE   CR 7

Male human ranger 2/rogue 5

CN Medium humanoid

Init +3; **Senses** Listen +9, Spot +9

DEFENSE

AC 13, touch 13, flat-footed 10
   (+3 Dex)

hp 37 (currently 0; 2d8+5d6+7)

Fort +5, **Ref** +10, **Will** +0

Defensive Abilities evasion, trap sense +1,
   uncanny dodge

OFFENSE

Spd 30 ft.

Melee unarmed strike +8 (1d3 nonlethal)

Special Attacks favored enemy (giants +2),
   sneak attack +3d6

TACTICS

During Combat Kaven is most comfortable wielding
   small and fast weapons like daggers, short swords,
   or rapiers. In battle, he seeks out wounded foes,
   leaving stronger enemies for his "allies" to handle.

Morale Kaven is a coward at heart, but his worries—that
   abandoning his "allies" too soon would reveal the depths
   of his treachery—keep him in a fight longer than he might otherwise
   remain. If brought below 10 hit points, he feigns death with a Bluff
   check, hoping to seize a chance to escape once attentions are
   focused elsewhere. If this tactic fails, he gives in to his fear and
   makes a run for it. Kaven's already betrayed his allies once, and if
   he thinks betraying the PCs might aid in his own survival, he won't
   hesitate for a moment.

STATISTICS

Str 10, **Dex** 16, **Con** 12, **Int** 13, **Wis** 8, **Cha** 14

Base Atk +5; **Grp** +5

Feats Persuasive, Track, Two-Weapon Defense, Two-Weapon Fighting,
   Weapon Finesse

Skills Bluff +14, Climb +10, Hide +13, Intimidate +6, Listen +9,
   Move Silently +13, Search +11, Sleight of Hand +13, Spot +9,
   Survival +4, Swim +5

Languages Common, Giant

SQ trapfinding, wild empathy +4

KAVEN WINDSTRIKE

PART TWO: RETAKING RANNICK

Fort Rannick, as the PCs soon discover, has fallen. A notorious clan of ogres known as the Kreegs launched a devastating assault on the fort three weeks ago, an assault that left little doubt of treachery in the mind of the few survivors. Someone must have given the Kreegs detailed information about the fort's defenses—the assault was too perfect in its execution and timing for any other explanation to make sense.

After the PCs rescue the three remaining Black Arrows from the Grauls, they can tell the PCs how they arrived at the fort near the end of the battle, and that their attempt to retake the fort resulted in a disastrous rout that had the Black Arrow patrol fleeing for its life into Kreegwood. Their capture by the Grauls was practically guaranteed, but now that they've been rescued, the three Black Arrows are in need of leadership and support.

If the PCs make clear their intentions to try to retake Fort Rannick, all three Black Arrows pledge their assistance to the effort (Kaven must make a Bluff check to put on a brave face at this point—if he fails, the PCs might be able to uncover his treachery early). If the PCs don't come up with the idea of retaking the fort on their own, Vale eventually suggests the audacious plan. If the PCs contact Magnimar with the news, they're asked to, at the very least, scout the region and gather intelligence about the ogres now occupying the fort. If they can retake the fort, Lord-Mayor Grobaras implies that there could be a healthy reward for the PCs. In any event, the news encourages Magnimar to organize a large force to travel to the region to provide aid, but unfortunately winter has other plans. Heavy winds, rains, and even snow all but lock down easy travel around central Varisia—as a result, it will be several weeks before reinforcements arrive, and by then, Barl Breakbones and the Kreegs will be on the move.

Fort Rannick

Fort Rannick is located at the northern end of a wide valley that runs along the southern edge of the mountains. This bleak landscape stretches on for miles along the border between the mountains and Kreegwood. This rugged, forlorn landscape fits well with the morose and grim attitude of its guardians, the Order of the Black Arrow.

Vale can provide the PCs with a detailed map of Fort Rannick well in advance, so they should be able to plan their invasion of the fort as they wish. The Black Arrows provide answers to any questions about locations that the PCs have, including the presence of the shocker lizards in areas **B37** (they're unaware that one of their ancestors has risen from the dead in area

B15, though). Of course, they don't know where the ogres are located, or exactly how many ogres are still stationed within the fort. They can all but guarantee that there's a lot. While the ogres have the advantage of numbers, the PCs have the advantage of surprise and superior knowledge of the area—the rangers are positive that the ogres haven't discovered the secret caverns or tunnels, for example.

Infiltrating the Fort

The PCs are free to explore any means of gaining access to the fort they wish, down to a full frontal assault on the main gates if they like (though such an assault is likely suicidal). A few options (and likely suggestions from the Black Arrows or Shalelu if the PCs ask them) include:

The Sluice Gate: On the south wall of the fort, a sluice gate opens to release refuse and sewage downhill into the creek. The PCs can attempt to circumvent the gates of Rannick by breaching this narrow access way instead, but its proximity to the South Gate might be a problem.

The Secret Tunnels: These tunnels have not been used in decades. They are infested in some places by shocker lizards, but they might provide the perfect means of infiltrating the fort without alerting the ogres. The tunnels can be entered via the waterfall cave at area **B12**; from there, the PCs can infiltrate the fort via the secret entrances into areas **B10**, **B5**, or even **B36**.

Death from Above: Any PC capable of flight can descend on the fort proper from above. Alternatively, if they fly up to the eagle aerie (see area **B5**), they can approach the fort via the hidden ledge and tunnel from the north.

Stealth: Ogres can see in the dark, so night is likely to be a bigger problem than advantage for the PCs. If the party consists of stealthy characters, they might be able to infiltrate the fort undetected, especially if they use spells like *invisibility* or *fog cloud* to mask their approach.

Trickery: The ogres recognize the Sihedron Rune as the mark of their new lord, Barl Breakbones. If the PCs march brazenly into the keep and act as if they belong there and openly display the rune, the ogres assume they are envoys sent by Barl to check up on them and quickly lead them into the keep interior to meet with "The Boss" (Jaagrath in area **B29**) or "The Lady" (Lucrecia in area **B36**). How the PCs handle their likely short-lived fame with the ogres is left to them, as neither Jaagrath nor Lucrecia is foolish enough to fall for this ruse for long.

Attack Plans

The following tidbits of information are available to PCs based on skill checks or by asking the right questions of the Black Arrows. In the event that an attack plan goes wrong, the PCs should not discount the option of retreating, regrouping, and attacking again. The ogres are disorganized, lazy, and slow to rouse in an organized defense, and even if a fight turns noisy, nearby ogres are prone to assume it's just another argument between brothers. Since there are approximately three dozen ogres in the fort, fighting them all at once is a poor tactic.

The New Barracks: Area **B10** is known as the "new barracks," even though they were built 20 years ago. Erected when the rangers grew concerned that Fort Rannick was going to outgrow its original barracks space, the wooden barracks (though spacious and less dank than the quarters in area **B20** and **B24**) were abandoned after it was pointed out they were deathtraps: if fire were used during a siege, the barracks would go up like tinder and everyone inside would burn to death. The ogres are not so observant or knowledgeable, and a good number of their hulking brood make their quarters here—using fire on this building would likely kill several of them and distract the others long enough for an infiltration elsewhere. A character who spends an hour observing the fort from afar can make a DC 20 Knowledge (architecture and engineering) check to realize this. Alternatively, the PCs can hit upon this tactic by asking the Black Arrows about using fire to assault the ogres.

Lure the Kreegs Out: While Jaagrath is not stupid, the same can't be said for most of the other ogres in the fort. They are easily angered, quick to action, and not prone to evaluating threats before they act. If something provokes the ogres, they are likely to send out a sizeable force to attack (and could be easily lured into an ambush). Additionally, a distraction in one area of the fort might draw the brunt of the ogres to this area to investigate, thus leaving others undefended.

Smoke Out!: If the PCs ask about the creatures that infest the secret tunnels, the rangers can confirm that a large number of shocker lizards dwell down there. They keep to themselves in the tunnels, mostly, but during their mating seasons when they grow more aggressive, the rangers use bitterbark smoke to sicken and repulse them, keeping them from overrunning the castle. It takes a day and a DC 18 Knowledge (nature) check to harvest bitterbark from the surrounding region, but if the PCs do so and stage the smoke at the right places, they could possibly drive the shocker lizards up into the keep and into the ogres' midst, weakening them and allowing a greater chance to get at the leaders.

Fort Rannick

The slovenly ogres have turned this battle-worn but well-run fort into a charnel house of slaughter and drunken debauchery. The Kreegs did their best to make their initial captives last, but recently, the last of their living playthings perished and they've been spreading out, searching outlying areas for new victims to torment and eventually eat. Dozens of skulls and mangled corpses hang from trees near the fort, gigantic rusty hooks spitting them like meat awaiting a butcher's block. The stench of sweat, urine, blood, and ogre-musk befouls the air for hundreds of yards around the fort. Hulking deformed brutes of the Kreeg clan roam the walls of Rannick and lurk within, fatting themselves on human flesh, slaking their thirst on the Black Arrows' stores of whisky and ale, and dancing their macabre skull-jigs.

B1. Approach

A thunderbolt shakes the stone and earth underfoot, its low growl echoing through the valley. Talons of lightning claw at the sky, casting pale light on the mountainside below. The lightning storm reveals a grim fortress of dark gray stone standing sentinel over the valley, huddled desperately at the base of two sheer cliffsides. Crumbling, fifteen-foot-high walls ring the citadel, the stone pitted and cratered from hurled boulders and ogre hooks. Like the face of a veteran with decades of winters under his belt, the fort's craters, cracks, and scars are testament to its battle-weary history. A stone keep, a stubborn shadow against the mountainside, rises from behind the worn walls, a single tower jutting up from its ramparts like an ugly broken tooth. Nearby, a rushing curtain of white water cascades down the mountainside into a large pool of water just outside the fort's walls.

The fort's 15-foot-high wall is battered and chipped, offering plenty of hand- and footholds. A DC 15 Climb check is sufficient to scamper over the wall, but bits of rubble break free in the process, imparting a –5 penalty on Move Silently checks made while climbing. The nameless creek that runs along the perimeter of the walls like a moat is 10 feet deep but relatively placid, requiring a DC 10 Swim check to cross.

B2. East Gate (EL 3)

A twenty-foot-tall gatehouse surrounds two battered wooden double doors that look as if they're barely hanging on their hinges.

The ogres smashed this gate on their initial assault, but have since mounded up debris and junk on the other side to fortify it. Until the rubble is cleared, these doors won't open.

Creature: Since the Kreegs assume they've completely blocked this gate, only one ogre is posted here, busily scrubbing at a freshly claimed skull to polish it to a fine sheen. He takes a –4 on his Spot checks as a result.

OGRE   **CR 3**
hp 29 (MM 199)

B3. Stable

A large wooden building sits against the cliffside here. The structure's southern facade is open, revealing an empty stable.

A proud herd of fine horses bred and kept by the Black Arrows was once stabled here. The brave animals detected trouble in the fort the night of the massacre and several smashed free of their stalls to rush to their masters' aid, only to be massacred by the ogres.

B4. Old Guard Tower (EL 8)

This old tower is falling apart. Most of the mortar has cracked or sloughed away, leaving stone to grind on stone. The structure itself is nearly thirty feet high.

Abandoned by the Black Arrows due to its unsafe condition, the ogres don't realize how close to collapse this tower is. The tower itself has hardness 8, but if any single attack manages to deal a mere 15 points of damage to it, the entire structure collapses. Any creatures inside the tower take 10d6 points of damage when it collapses, while any creature within 15 feet takes 6d6 points of damage (DC 15 Reflex save for half). Collapsing the tower brings all of the ogres from areas **B2**, **B6**, **B8**, and **B10** running, leaving those areas unguarded for 2d6 minutes.

Creatures: The ogres, not known for their powers of observation, have stationed three of their number here. Two are unexceptional ogre thugs, while the third is a sick, grunting thing with knees that bend in reverse like a goat and a host of angry red pustules covering his face and hands. This horror, Karly-Lop Kreeg, spends most of his time tormenting the other two ogres—all three of them take a –4 penalty on Listen and Spot checks.

KARLY-LOP KREEG   **CR 7**
hp 79 (MM 199, ogre barbarian)

OGRES (2)   **CR 3**
hp 29 each (MM 199)

Treasure: Karly-Lop wears a necklace of shriveled women's hands about his neck, each adorned with shiny copper rings. Of the rings, 21 are worth 10 gp each, while the 22nd is actually a *ring of animal friendship* (though Karly-Lop has no idea it is magical).

B5. Collapsed Tunnel

A huge pile of rubble slumps against the cliff face here, almost completely blocking a cave entrance.

The tunnel beyond winds up to a ledge that overlooks the fort, 120 feet up the cliff face above. This ledge rises a further 450 feet to a tor that once served as the nesting ground for a group of giant eagles allied with the Black Arrows. The eagles swooped down to aid the fort in defense against the ogres, but all were slain.

There's enough room for a Tiny creature to squeeze through the gap into the tunnel; a Small creature can do the same with a DC 30 Escape Artist check. Clearing away enough rubble to make room for a Medium creature takes 3d6 minutes of noisy work.

B6. Cook House (EL 7)

This open-air structure contains several large racks for storing smoked meat. The ogres don't seem to have taken good care of the place, for everything is in a jumbled, broken ruin now. Several dead bodies lie haphazardly on the damaged smokers, slowly (and inefficiently) curing as the fires smolder. The smell is disturbingly flavorful.

Ogres love a good barbeque. The nine bodies slow-roasting here were all Black Arrows captured alive—they didn't last long once they were threaded onto skewers and left here to cook, though.

To Aeries of the Eagles

B15
S
B5
B4
B3
B14
B2
B1
B6
B11
To B37
B10
S
B13
B8
B7
B12
B9

Fort Rannick

One square = 20 feet

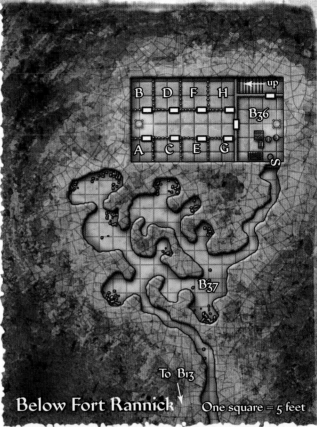

B D F H
up
B36
A C E G
S

B37

To B13

Below Fort Rannick

One square = 5 feet

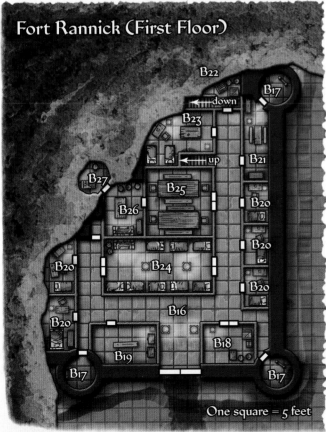

Fort Rannick (First Floor)

B22
B17
down
B23
up
B21
B27
B25
B20
B26
B20
B20
B24
B20
B16
B20
B18
B20
B19
B17
B17

One square = 5 feet

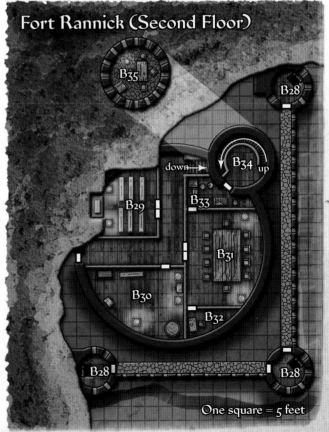

Fort Rannick (Second Floor)

B35
B28
down
B34
up
B33
B29
B31
B30
B32
B28
B28

One square = 5 feet

Creatures: Jaagrath put his best cook in charge of this project, a constantly wheezing and sweating obese ogre named Jolly Kreeg. With tiny little hands and feet and a grotesquely oversized head and rear end, the ogre almost looks like a bulbous gourd. Jolly is currently making a big batch of dough to bake up the entrails he's just extracted from the smoking corpses in a huge "gutworm pie" for Jaagrath.

Jolly Kreeg   CR 7

hp 79 (MM 199, ogre barbarian)

B7. Drainage Ditch

A vile pool of sewage sits at the base of a nook in the wall. The pool drains through a two-foot-wide sluiceway in the wall to the creek beyond, but a body is lodged head-first inside it.

The body is one of the rangers of Fort Rannick, his head claimed for Jaagrath's grotesque collection, the rest of him deposited carelessly here. The ogres never bothered to kick him through the sluice, and have taken to calling the bloating corpse "Spongy." The sluiceway is slick with reeking gore, algae, and waste. A Small creature can clamber through it easily, but a Medium creature must make a DC 20 Escape Artist check to do the same. Pushing aside the body wedged in the opening requires a DC 18 Strength check. A character that attempts to enter the fort via this route must make a DC 12 Fortitude save to avoid catching filth fever.

B8. South Gate (EL 9)

This twenty-foot-tall gatehouse is protected by an iron portcullis.

The ogres left this entrance relatively undamaged, since this is the one they use to come and go from the fort. The mechanism to lift the portcullis is located atop the defense platform directly west of the gate—it takes five rounds to raise the portcullis, but a DC 28 Strength check allows someone to lift it from the ground.

Creatures: Since this gate is still functional, more ogres are on guard here. Four stand on watch in all—three average ogres led by Minktuck Kreeg, an unfortunate ogre who lost most of his lower jaw in a fight many years ago. He's taken to fixing freshly shucked minks (head, paws, and all) onto each jowl every few weeks, so the little dead animals dangle and bounce about freakishly as he slobbers out orders. Minktuck keeps his ogres focused and relatively alert; these ogres do not take distraction penalties on their Listen and Spot checks as a result.

Minktuck Kreeg   CR 8

Male ogre fighter 5

CE Large giant

Init +0; **Senses** darkvision 60 ft., low-light vision; Listen +3, Spot +3

DEFENSE

AC 19, touch 9, flat-footed 19

  (+5 armor, +5 natural, –1 size)

hp 90 (4d8+5d10+45)

Fort +15, **Ref** +2, **Will** +3

OFFENSE

Spd 30 ft.

Melee +1 ogre hook +16/+11 (3d6+13/19–20/×3)

Ranged mwk composite longbow +8/+3 (2d6+7/×3)

Space 10 ft.; **Reach** 10 ft.

TACTICS

During Combat Minktuck begins combat using his bow, but drops the paltry ranged weapon to use his ogre hook at the first opportunity.

Morale If brought below 20 hit points, Minktuck abandons the fort and tries to flee into the mountains.

STATISTICS

Str 24, **Dex** 11, **Con** 20, **Int** 6, **Wis** 12, **Cha** 4

Base Atk +8; **Grp** +19

Feats Cleave, Great Fortitude, Improved Bull Rush, Improved Critical (ogre hook), Power Attack, Weapon Focus (ogre hook), Weapon Specialization (ogre hook)

Skills Climb +15, Listen +3, Spot +3

Languages Common, Giant

Combat Gear potion of cure moderate wounds; **Other Gear** +1 hide shirt, +1 ogre hook, masterwork composite longbow (+7 Str) with 20 arrows

Ogres (3)   CR 3

hp 29 each (MM 199)

B9. Pond

What once might have been a crystal-clear mountain lake has become an abattoir. Partially butchered and mutilated bodies, some human, some horse, some giant eagle, lie sprawled along the shore. A waterfall plummets from the cliffs to the west into the pool, which keeps much of the water clean save for near the shores where the dead lie thick.

This lake is the primary source of drinking water for the fort. The pool itself is 30 feet deep at its center. A cursory examination of the waterfall from afar (and a DC 30 Search check) allows a character to see a cave behind the cascade ten feet above the water. It's only a DC 10 Climb check to get up to the cave.

The ogres are unaware of this cave entrance, since they generally just drink right out of the stream when they're thirsty.

B10. New Barracks (EL 10)

This wooden building seems to have been abandoned for some time; it's in fairly poor repair and seems almost to lean against the cliff wall behind it for support. A short flight of wood steps lead up to the single door. The building itself sits on raised timbers over the uneven, sloping ground below—excess lumber is stored haphazardly in the space below.

These barracks were still called "new" by the older members of the order, though they were built 20 years ago. Constructed at a time when no sensible architect resided among the Black Arrows, the building is a deathtrap should it ever catch on fire. With the heavy rains, setting fire to the barracks from outside is a difficult task. A character who sneaks into the barracks, or who clambers under the building where all of the extra lumber is stored, can light a fire relatively easily. If the building burns, the ogres within panic at the single tiny exit, fight over who's supposed to escape first, and eventually cook inside the building.

The secret door in the base of the cliff wall behind this building can be found with a DC 25 Search check.

Creatures: Many of the ogres balked at sleeping in the main keep, opting instead to shack up in this nice unused barrack ("No man-stink! Who wants to smell food all night long while sleeping?"). The bulk of the raiding party's ogres can be found here, sleeping, eating, or arguing—a dozen in all.

OGRES (12)   **CR 3**
hp 29 each (MM 199)

B11. Entrance to Fort Rannick

A single set of double doors allows entrance to the central keep of Fort Rannick. The doors are made of oak and have been brutally battered and savaged. Crude repairs have been effected, but the doors still hang somewhat askew.

The ogres did their best to repair these doors, but until an actual skilled carpenter works on them, they'll remain in sad condition. They cannot be locked, but they don't open easily—it takes a DC 16 Strength check to pry them open. The entrance leads to area **B16**.

B12. Waterfall Cave

The floor of this cave is dotted with puddles. Patches of pale moss and fungus grow in sheets on the wall, while to the north, a five-foot-wide passageway angles up into darkness. A walkway of soggy planks leads from this opening southeast to a second opening curtained by cascades of falling water.

Apart from the wooden walkway, the floor in this cave is slippery, requiring a DC 12 Balance check to navigate.

B13. Secret Armory (EL 4)

The floor, walls, and ceiling of this cool, damp cave are coated from floor to ceiling in soft, dark gray fungus. Several crates are stacked in a nook to the northwest.

This cave was used by the Black Arrows to store additional weapons in the event of a siege. Unfortunately, the ogres' assault on the keep came with such sudden force that none of the Black

Arrows were able to reach this armory in time to make use of the weapons kept in the crates.

A passageway to the east leads to a secret door that opens out behind the new barracks. Just before this door, a side-passage winds down under the central keep, connecting to area **B37**.

Creatures: Two shocker lizards, wanderers from the larger colony in area **B37**, have come up here to look for more food. They squeal in surprise when they see the PCs, hanging around only long enough to generate a lethal shock before they attempt to flee to the east and back to area **B37**.

SHOCKER LIZARDS (2)   **CR 2**
hp 13 each (MM 224)

Treasure: Apart from a fair supply of mundane weapons (including two dozen longswords, shortswords, daggers, and longbows), one of the crates contains an oilcloth wrapped around six *+2 shocking burst arrows*.

B14. Ravine (EL 3)

A deep ravine stretches across this cavern, splitting the room in half. Geodes and veins of glittering minerals shimmer along the walls of the chasm, which drops away into the dark. A ten-foot-wide wooden bridge spans the gulf.

The gems glittering along the walls of the chasm, while pretty and shiny, are relatively worthless rock crystal. They do make the walls of the 50-foot-deep chasm very slick and difficult to climb, though—it's a DC 25 Climb check to scale these walls.

Trap: The bridge itself is in poor condition, since the Black Arrows rarely used it. If more than one Medium creature attempts to cross it at the same time, the bridge collapses.

COLLAPSING BRIDGE   **CR 3**
Type mechanical
Search DC 20; **Disable Device** DC 25

EFFECTS

Trigger location; **Reset** repair
Effect fall (50 feet, 5d6, Reflex DC 20 negates); multiple targets
    (10-ft. middle section of bridge)

Treasure: The skeleton of an unlucky halfling thief lies at the bottom of the ravine. His pack contains a broken flask, some prospecting tools, and a pouch with two large rubies each worth 100 gp. His trusty *+1 silver short sword* is still sheathed at his side.

B15. Crypt (EL 7)

The walls of this fairly dry cavern contain twenty seven-foot-wide, two-foot-high niches, in each of which rests the ancient body of a long-dead humanoid. The skeletons wear ceremonial armor and weapons of various types. One of the bodies has been pulled from its niche and lies in a tangled jumble on the ground to the north.

This is where the Black Arrows once interred the remains of their brothers and sisters. The crypt filled far more quickly than the Black Arrows anticipated, and rather than spend more time expanding the crypt, they began sending off their fallen kin in elaborate pyres and then scattering the ashes. No Black Arrow has been buried in this crypt for nearly 30 years—which is unfortunate, since the last body they interred here has not rested peacefully.

The armor and weapons the bodies are buried with are ceremonial only—ever thrifty, the Black Arrows recycle their members' weapons after death.

Creatures: The last Black Arrow buried here was a bitter, brutal man named Lorgus Fenker. His "accident" while on patrol was rightly suspected of being an arrangement made between the others in his group, but since the leaders of the order at the time felt that his passing was for the best, there was little investigation into the particulars behind his fatal fall from a ledge up on the Hook.

Fenker was indeed murdered by his brethren, and his bitter, surly soul rose from the dead a week after he was buried here (several days after the order decided to quit using the crypt). He exists now as a spectre, bound to this crypt by the presence of his bones. He cannot stray further than the confines of this chamber, but anyone who dares intrude shall feel his wrath.

LORGUS FENKER   CR 7
Spectre
hp 45 (MM 232)

B16. Main Hall

What might once have been a well-maintained entrance hall is now swathed in horror. Dried blood cakes the stone walls; bits and pieces of armor, weaponry, and flesh litter the floor; and flies cloud the air. Tapestries that once bore the insignia of the Black Arrows have been torn from the walls and now lie on the floor in shreds, coated with filth.

The keep is old, its masonry battered by the elements for hundreds of years. The walls are worn and chipped in many places and significantly weakened. Ceiling height in the main keep averages twelve feet—high enough that most of the Kreegs within don't need to stoop.

B17. Towers

Each of these featureless round rooms contains a ladder that can be used to access a trap door in the ceiling above (area **B28**). The ogres are too ungainly to navigate these ladders.

B18. Workroom (EL 8)

The lathes, sawhorses, and other tools in this workroom lie in scattered, shattered ruin on the floor. The walls are smeared with gore, in some places forming messy graffiti.

The graffiti, written in Giant, includes such phrases as: "Me Big-a-Big, You-Small-a-Small, I Eat Your Head!" and "You Never

Think Me Write All Over With You Bloody Neck, I'm Holding You by Mig-a-Mug and Use You as Paint Brush! Har!"

Creature: The happy painter of these verses is taking a break from his work to chew on the mangled, decapitated body of his latest paintbrush. One of the few literate Kreegs, this is Gragavan, an ogre who fancies himself something of a poet. Shortly after taking the keep, Gragavan found that one of the Black Arrows, a lanky mumbling simpleton named Petter, kept a diary of utterly inane "poetry" that proved even more puerile than his own. He promptly hooked off the ranger's head and has been using his putrefying corpse as a calligraphy brush ever since. He laughs and hurls Petter at the PCs when he notices them, then draws his weapon and goes to bloody work.

GRAGAVAN KREEG   CR 8
Male ogre fighter 5
hp 90 (see page 28)

B19. Armory (EL 5)

This large room is filled chiefly with several heavy wooden racks, all bristling with pikes, longswords, and quivers of barbed arrows. The wall where the door once was has been smashed in, and rubble litters the floor.

Creatures: Two ogres are at play here, trying on man-sized suits of armor and helmets, guffawing at each other in the "tiny man clothes" and then shuffling about in them. The two have also started their own collection of heads mounted on the pikes here. Every couple of days, Jaagrath stops by to examine the new additions, claiming the best of the skulls these two have gathered, much to their chagrin. If they hear battle in the keep, they run out, still bedecked in tiny clinging suits of armor and with silly miniscule helms balanced on their giant heads, to join the fray.

OGRES (2)   CR 3
hp 29 each (MM 199)

B20. Guest Quarters

These rooms are where the Black Arrows quartered guests, trainees, and other visitors. The ogres have tossed all of these rooms but haven't bothered to go out of their way to ruin the furniture—yet.

B21. Library

A long table with benches to either side sits in this room opposite a bookshelf filled with dozens of books, most of which have been torn from the shelves, mangled, and then messily stuffed back in place.

The rangers used this room as a place to keep important documents about their order, atlases, bestiaries, and other books that held their interest.

B22. Storeroom

Crates, barrels, and a stack of firewood have been smashed apart and heaped in a tangled pile in the corner of this room. A flight of stairs leads down to the west.

Nothing of value remains in the ruined containers. The stairs double back on themselves after a landing before reaching area **B36** below.

B23. Infirmary (EL 8)

Once used to house the wounded and sick, this chamber is now a slice of some blood-drenched nightmare. Hacked pieces of bodies litter the sick beds. The floor is slick with gore, strewn with mangled organs and heaps of entrails. A dead fat man sits at one of the operating tables, arranged as if he were merrily spooning chunks of his own disembodied organs out of a brown bowl. His guts spill out of a large gaping slash in his midsection.

Creatures: One of Jaagrath's own sons, an unfortunately handsome ogre named Silas, resides here. Although Silas's body resembles his hulking father, his face was strangely symmetrical and free of warts, bonespurs, and gristle—far too pretty for Jaagrath's liking. Jaagrath shaved off the entire right side of Silas' face, leaving a pulped ruin with skull showing through in places. Every week or so, Jaagrath "fixes" his son's face with his hook, keeping him looking "right." Silas was the first over the wall on the night of the massacre, taking his own ogre hook to the necks of the sleeping rangers in the barracks even before the alarm was raised.

Silas has a bit of a cruel artistic streak in him—his medium is death. The fat man, once a cleric of Erastil who dwelt here, is his latest masterpiece. Silas changes his pose two or three times a day, often inviting other ogres in so he can make them admire his work and shower him with praise.

SILAS KREEG   **CR 8**
Male ogre fighter 5
hp 90 (see page 28)

B24. Barracks (EL 7)

These once-well-appointed barracks are now filled with nothing but splintered bunks and tables. The west wall is completely demolished, with bits of its masonry scattered about.

Creatures: Four ogres squat and squabble here, constantly arguing over who gets to wear the hollowed-out horse head Grothrak made. Grothrak was murdered by his kinsfolk when he refused to share his "horsey-mask." Five other ogres have since died in heated battles over the "funny" horse head. If the PCs find a way to exacerbate the argument (perhaps using stealth or magic to place the horse head into one ogre's sack, or using

magic to compel one to claim it for himself), these remaining ogres snatch up clubs and rusty hooks and murder each other with relish.

OGRES (4)   **CR 3**
hp 29 each (MM 199)

B25. Mess Hall

This ramshackle area is a mess of smashed tables, broken crockery, and rubble. No living thing stirs here.

Once where the rangers took their meals, this chamber is now just another demolished room.

B26. Kitchen

This kitchen is in shambles, as if a cyclone had moved through the room, smashed every bit of furniture, bent every bit of silverware, and partially collapsed the stone fireplace.

When they cook their food, the ogres prefer to use methods like those on display at the cook house (area **B6**). This room held their interest for a few hours, but now they've abandoned it.

B27. Pantry

All that remains in this room is a half-smashed crate and an untouched barrel.

The ogres raided this pantry early in their stay, moving most of the food into the kitchen to sort. The barrel to the north contains pickled fish—a delicacy the smell of which the ogres simply can't stomach.

B28. Ramparts

These stone platforms are shielded by crenellations spaced at even intervals, offering those behind them cover against archer fire and a perfect killing angle on foes charging the keep below.

B29. Chapel (EL 10)

The walls within this enormous chamber are mounted with dozens of trophy antlers, some taken from stags that must have stood as tall as dire bears. Most of the antlers are draped with bits of rotten flesh, strips of skin, or coils of viscera. To the west, a marble altar has been heaped with the mangled remains of at least a half-dozen dead men and women. A crude image of what might be a three-eyed jackal has been painted in blood on the wall above the altar's alcove.

This chapel, once dedicated to Erastil, was a place of worship for the Black Arrows—the antlers on the wall being trophies offered up to the god of the hunt. The shrine has been thoroughly defiled in every way by the ogres, converted into a makeshift altar to Lamashtu, goddess of monsters.

Creatures: Jaagrath, the dread "pappy" of the Kreegs, awaits the PCs here. He doesn't respond to the sounds of violence elsewhere, assuming his deranged brood can quell any threat. He quietly and calmly sits here, creating taxidermy terrors out of dead rangers, horses, bits of giant eagle, and the many antlers found here. His "masterpieces" hang about the room on bloody hooks—men with eagle heads sewn to their bodies, a horse with a woman's face where its own face once drooped, dead men with huge sets of antlers jutting from their bodies, and men with stags' heads and hooves.

Jaagrath Kreeg is "pappy" by blood but also by might. He stands easily 14 feet in height and his arms are the size of the Mushfens' largest boa constrictors. He squeezes the life out of foes face-to-face, casually gnawing off cheeks and lips so their screams resonate through his skull (he likes the funny buzzing their cries make in his head). He maintains dominance over the rest of his kin through a number of brutal means ranging from rape to mutilation. None dare disobey his commands.

JAAGRATH KREEG   CR 10

Male ogre barbarian 7

CE Large giant

Init +1; **Senses** darkvision 60 ft., low-light vision; Listen +8, Spot +1

DEFENSE

AC 15, touch 8, flat-footed 14

(+2 armor, +1 Dex, +5 natural, –2 rage, –1 size)

hp 118 (4d8+7d12+55)

Fort +14, **Ref** +4, **Will** +4

Defensive Abilities trap sense +2, improved uncanny dodge; **DR** 1/—

OFFENSE

Spd 50 ft.

Melee +1 human bane ogre hook +21/+16 (3d6+16/19–20/×3)

Space 10 ft.; **Reach** 10 ft.

Special Attacks rage 2/day

TACTICS

During Combat Jaagrath is perhaps a bit overconfident in his fighting prowess, but that certainly doesn't mean he's a pushover. He rages on the first round of combat, then focuses his attacks on humans, saving other races for "clean up." On the first round of combat, he makes full Power Attacks (+11/+6; 3d6+36/19–20/×3), but if he misses he drops his Power Attack bonus by 5 points, and then entirely if he continues to miss.

Morale If Jaagrath is brought below 25 hit points, he attempts to flee to area **B30** to recruit aid, drinking both of his potions as soon as he gets a chance. Once at area **B30**, he fights to the death.

Base Statistics When Jaagrath isn't raging, his stats change as follows:

    AC 17, touch 10, flat-footed 16

    hp 96

    Fort +12, **Will** +2

    Melee +1 human bane ogre hook +19/+14 (3d6+13/19–20/×3)

    Str 26, **Con** 16

    Skills Climb +11

STATISTICS

Str 30, **Dex** 12, **Con** 20, **Int** 6, **Wis** 8, **Cha** 9

Base Atk +10; **Grp** +22

Feats Improved Bull Rush, Improved Critical (ogre hook), Power Attack, Weapon Focus (ogre hook)

Skills Climb +13, Intimidate +6, Listen +8, Spot +1

Languages Common, Giant

Combat Gear potions of cure serious wounds (2); **Other Gear** +1 human bane ogre hook, bracers of armor +2, belt of giant strength +4

Development: If the PCs defeat Jaagrath and think to use his head or his ogre hook as a trophy to intimidate the other ogres, they gain a +15 bonus on Intimidate checks. If an Intimidate check beats its required DC by 10, those ogres panic, and rather than taking a penalty on attack rolls, they flee Fort Rannick entirely. Once at least three groups of ogres flee, word spreads and all the remaining ogres abandon the fort as well.

JAAGRATH KREEG

BOOTS OF THE MIRE

Aura faint abjuration and transmutation; **CL** 5th

Slot boots; **Price** 3,500 gp

DESCRIPTION

These soft leather boots confer several powers upon the wearer. First, he is granted the power to walk on water in swamp environments, provided the water is no deeper than five feet—this effectively lets him move through swampy terrain and mud at no cost to his speed. He leaves no tracks or other sign of his passage as long as he's in swampy terrain, and prevent him from becoming uncomfortable or wet from rain, fog, and other precipitation. Finally, the boots grant him a +2 resistance bonus on Fortitude saves against poison and disease.

CONSTRUCTION

Requirements Craft Wondrous Item; *endure elements, pass without trace, resistance, water walk*; **Cost** 1,750 gp, 140 XP

B30. Commander's Quarters (EL 11)

The walls of this room are decorated with fine longswords, stuffed animal heads, and a map of the Hook Mountain environs. A large oak table surrounded by several chairs has been smashed to splinters, and an immense bed has similarly been ruined. An open cabinet that once contained several bottles of wine has been crushed as well, and broken bottles and the faint scent of wine linger around its ruins.

This is where the commander of the Black Arrows, a gallant ranger named Lamatar, resided. Lamatar's fate is far worse than death—captured alive by the ogres, he was dragged back to Hook Mountain in chains, but not before his longtime lover, a beautiful nymph named Myriana, came to his aid and attempted to free him. She failed and was torn to pieces before his eyes. More horrors were yet to come. Lamatar was tortured unspeakably at the Kreeg clanhold, and then eventually transformed into a wight and turned over to the Three Sisters of Winter's Heart as payment for the hags' services in engineering the storms that have wracked the region.

Creatures: The current occupant of this chamber is Jaagrath's mistress and seer, a sorcerer named Dorella. The ogress is attended in turn by one of her lovers, Harlock "Hookmaw" Kreeg. Hookmaw is Jaagrath's son and half-brother. Jaagrath tortured the boy day and night when he was young, and when he came of age, as a special rite of passage, papa pulled his teeth and replaced them with a specially forged set of metal teeth strapped to his face by a too-tight leather harness that squeezes his skull tortuously.

Dorella Kreeg herself is Jaagrath's daughter and wife. Dorella is the only spellcaster among the Kreegs, and is both feared and prized by her kin. The ogres believe she's got the "touch o' spirits," granting her magic powers. Dorella had her head bashed in by one of her dozens of brothers when she was young. She "ain't never been right" since, but the nearly fatal head wound has seemed to grant her a strange gift with magic.

DORELLA KREEG   CR 10

Female ogre sorcerer 9

CE Large giant

Init −1; **Senses** darkvision 60 ft., low-light vision; Listen +5, Spot +4

DEFENSE

AC 19, touch 8, flat-footed 19

   (+4 armor, −1 Dex, +7 natural, −1 size)

hp 92 (4d8+9d4+52)

Fort +13, **Ref** +3, **Will** +10

OFFENSE

Spd 40 ft.

Melee dagger +10/+5 (1d6+4/19–20)

Space 10 ft.; **Reach** 10 ft.

Spells Known (CL 9th, +5 ranged touch)

   4th (4/day)—*confusion* (DC 18), *shout* (DC 16)

   3rd (6/day)—*deep slumber* (DC 17), *lightning bolt* (DC 15), *suggestion* (DC 17)

   2nd (7/day)—*blindness/deafness* (DC 14), *hideous laughter* (DC 16), *mirror image, touch of idiocy*

   1st (7/day)—*charm person* (DC 15), *mage armor, magic missile, shield, true strike*

   0 (6/day)—*acid splash, dancing lights, daze* (DC 14), *ghost sound* (DC 12), *mage hand, mending, message, prestidigitation*

TACTICS

Before Combat Dorella casts *mage armor* as soon as she suspects trouble's come to the fort.

During Combat While Hookmaw distracts the PCs, Dorella casts *shield* and *mirror image* before using her spells against them. She saves *shout* for when Hookmaw falls, hoping to attract the attention of reinforcements while at the same time damaging her foes.

Morale Dorella attempts to escape if brought below 20 hit points, after casting *confusion* to delay pursuit.

STATISTICS

Str 18, **Dex** 8, **Con** 18, **Int** 8, **Wis** 13, **Cha** 15

Base Atk +7; **Grp** +15

Feats Alertness (as long as It Tickles is in arm's reach), Eschew Materials, Extend Spell, Greater Spell Focus (enchantment), Iron Will, Spell Focus (enchantment)

Skills Climb +4, Concentration +13, Listen +5, Spot +4

Languages Common, Giant

SQ summon familiar (rat named It Tickles)

Combat Gear *wand of acid arrow* (43 charges); **Other Gear** dagger, *amulet of natural armor +2, cloak of Charisma +2*

GRAGAVAN KREEG   CR 8

Male ogre fighter 5

hp 90 (see page 28)

Treasure: Although the Kreegs have done a number on the contents of this room, they aren't quite observant enough to have noticed that the bottom of the wine cabinet contained a hidden compartment. Partially smashed open from the top, it's only a DC 15 Search check to notice the hidden compartment—the latch to open it is broken, so the thin slats of wood above

it must be pried away to expose what's hidden within—a flat wooden coffer, a pair of soft green leather boots, and a tiny jewelry box.

The coffer contains dozens and dozens of parchment sheets, all containing beautifully-written love sonnets to someone named "Myriana," who (if the sonnets are to be believed) is so beautiful that the moon itself was "blinded when it spied her dancing on the tarn," and that she is "the truest grace to know Whitewillow's soft embrace." A DC 30 Knowledge (geography) or Knowledge (local) check is enough to realize that "Whitewillow" is a section of the Shimmerglens said to be particularly close to one of the portals to the First Realm of the Fey.

The boots are *boots of the mire*, a new magical item detailed in the sidebar on page 33. The jewelry box contains a silver locket on a chain; inside the locket is a lock of silky golden hair. A DC 22 Knowledge (nature) check is enough to identify the hair as having come from a nymph.

All three of these items are surprises to any of the surviving Black Arrows—none of them knew Lamatar had a poetic side, and certainly none of them knew anything about him having a mistress. After a few minutes of thought, both Vale and Jakardros agree that Lamatar did often leave Fort Rannick for two to three days at a time, once a month, on what he called

his "communion walks," lone treks made through the region to supposedly put him closer to the realm he had been charged to guard. It's certainly possible the ex-commander had been using these walks as a cover for monthly visits to a secret paramour.

In fact, this is exactly the case—Lamatar had long been involved in a secret affair with the caretaker of Whitewillow, a nymph princess named Myriana. The repercussions of this affair, his death, and Myriana's tragic attempt to rescue him from the Kreegs is detailed in Part Four.

B31. Tribunal (EL 5)

Smashed chairs and a ruined table sit in this once-regal chamber. Along the curved east wall hang tattered remnants of several regional maps.

Creatures: Two ogres have hung three Black Arrow ranger corpses from the rafters here, and are in the process of bleeding them into grimy buckets. When they detect intruders, they kick aside the buckets and, with cries of rage, leap forward to attack.

OGRES (2)   CR 3

hp 29 each (MM 199)

B32. Map Room

Wood and glass cases lay in ruins, hundreds of sheaves of parchment within now spilled about, spattered in blood and torn to shreds.

Treasure: This room contained dozens of maps of the Hook Mountain region and other Varisian locales. Now, only a few remain intact, one detailing several of the smugglers' tunnels beneath Riddleport (worth 50 gp to a smuggler), another detailing the first few poisonous levels of Viperwall (worth 400 gp to an interested party), and another of the hidden paths of Lurkwood's interior (worth 700 gp to explorers set on investigating the mist-shrouded woods, and likely of great use to the PCs later in *Pathfinder #5*'s "Sins of the Saviors").

B33. Storeroom

This room was used to store miscellaneous supplies and tools, but nothing of value remains now that the ogres are done with it.

B34. Tower Stairs

This flight of stairs ascends to the watchtower (area **B35**) above.

B35. Watchtower

A cracked bell hanging from a huge oak frame takes up most of this chamber's upper half. The ringer has been removed and replaced with an upside down dead ranger, a steel helm strapped tightly to his skull. A broken worktable and three chairs sit below, stained with the dead man's blood.

The ogres loved to play up here, smashing away at the bell with hammers and clubs day and night, until finally Jaagrath killed a few of them to ensure an end to the racket. If the PCs ring the bell, Jaagrath flies into a rage and leaves area **B29** to investigate, giving the PCs a good chance to catch the ogre commander off guard and perhaps corner him here where he can't easily escape.

B36. Lucrecia's Retreat (EL 7)

This simple room might have once been a jailer's den, or perhaps even a torture chamber, but someone has gone through great pains to repurpose it. The air now smells of sweet exotic incense, and veils of multi-colored silk drape from floor to ceiling throughout. Between the rustlings of the veils, glimpses of giant cushions are revealed. The floor is strewn with luxuriant soft red throw rugs and sheets.

Creatures: After abandoning her pleasure barge *Paradise* on the evening of the assault on Fort Rannick, the lamia matriarch Lucrecia made her way north to the keep to seek temporary quarters here. Jaagrath and his ogres recognized the *Sihedron medallion* she wore and were quick to offer her lodging in the fort while she waited for the rains and coming flood to finish the work she started in Turtleback Ferry.

Lucrecia prefers to spend her time in her humanoid form: an aristocratic-looking human woman with fire-red hair, and alabaster skin. Her face is pure elegance—high cheekbones, demure lust-stirring green eyes, and perfectly shaped eyebrows to accent them. Her true form is similar from the waist up, while from the waist down she has the body of an emerald green snake.

Lucrecia greets intruders with open arms and a smile—she has no confusion about the PCs being here to do her harm, but wants to offer them a chance to join her masters before she kills them—going so far as to say "Mokmurian would love to meet you!" If the PCs rebuff her, she shrugs coyly, assumes her true form, and attacks.

If Kaven is still with the PCs, Lucrecia can't resist twisting her dagger. When he reacts to her presence here with obvious guilt and shock, she sweetly compliments him on a job well done— "These oafish Kreegs would have had quite the trouble taking Rannick without the lovely details you provided us. Well done, my love!" She hopes to see the PCs tear the man apart—party strife does Lucrecia's cold heart good.

LUCRECIA CR 10

Lamia matriarch rogue 2 (*Pathfinder #2* 92)
Always CE Large monstrous humanoid (shapechanger)
Init +6; **Senses** darkvision 60 ft., low-light vision; Listen +3, Spot +3

DEFENSE

AC 28, touch 15, flat-footed 22
 (+4 armor, +6 Dex, +9 natural, −1 size)
hp 131 (12d8+2d6+70)
Fort +10, **Ref** +18, **Will** +12
Defensive Abilities evasion; **Immune** mind-affecting effects; **SR** 18

OFFENSE

Spd 40 ft., climb 40 ft., swim 40 ft.
Melee +1 keen rapier +17/+12/+7 (1d8+5/15–20 plus 1 Wisdom drain) and
 mwk dagger +17/+12 (1d6+2 plus 1 Wisdom drain) or
 touch +18 (2d4 Wisdom drain)
Space 10 ft.; **Reach** 5 ft.
Special Attacks sneak attack +1d6
Spell-Like Abilities (CL 10th)
 At will—*charm monster* (DC 21), *ventriloquism* (DC 18)
 3/day—*deep slumber* (DC 20), *dream, major image* (DC 20), *mirror image, suggestion* (DC 20)
Spells Known (CL 6th, +18 ranged touch)
 3rd (3/day)— *lightning bolt* (DC 19)
 2nd (5/day)—*hideous laughter* (DC 18), *undetectable alignment*
 1st (6/day)—*cure light wounds, divine favor, mage armor, shield*
 0 (6/day)—*dancing lights, daze* (DC 16), *detect magic, ghost sound* (DC 16), *mage hand, mending, prestidigitation*

TACTICS

Before Combat Lucrecia casts *mage armor* as soon as she becomes aware of trouble in the keep above (or in the shocker lizard caves in area **B37**). She starts every day with an *undetectable alignment* spell as well.
During Combat Lucrecia assumes her true form on the first round of

LUCRECIA

Fighting, Two-Weapon Fighting, Weapon Finesse

Skills Bluff +27, Climb +12, Concentration +20, Craft (tattooing) +13, Knowledge (arcana) +20, Knowledge (local) +22, Sense Motive +15, Spellcraft +22, Tumble +27, Swim +12, Use Magic Device +25

Languages Abyssal, Common, Draconic, Giant, Thassilonian

SQ alternate form, trapfinding

Combat Gear *wand of scorching ray* (22 charges); **Other Gear** *+1 keen rapier*, masterwork dagger, *Sihedron medallion* (+1 resistance bonus on all saves, *false life* as free action 1/day at CL 5th; see *Pathfinder #1* 55)

SPECIAL ABILITIES

Alternate Form (Su) A lamia matriarch has a single humanoid form that she can assume as a standard action—most lamia matriarchs have human, elven, or half-elven alternate forms. Their appearance in this form is identical from the waist up to their serpentine form, yet in humanoid form the lamia matriarch is Medium sized (−8 Strength, +2 Dex, −4 Constitution), cannot use her Wisdom drain attack, and has a base speed of 30 feet.

Wisdom Drain (Su) A lamia matriarch drains 1d6 points of Wisdom each time she hits with her melee touch attack. If she strikes a foe with a melee weapon, she drains 1 point of Wisdom instead. Unlike creatures with other kinds of ability drain attacks, a lamia matriarch does not heal damage when she uses her Wisdom drain.

Skills Lamia matriarchs have a +4 racial bonus on Bluff, Tumble, and Use Magic Device checks.

Spells Lamia matriarchs cast spells as 6th-level sorcerers, and can also cast spells from the cleric list. Cleric spells are considered arcane spells for a lamia matriarch, meaning that the creature doesn't need a divine focus to cast them.

B36a–B36h. Cells

These grimy, blood-spattered cells are empty save some fetid straw mats and vermin-ridden blankets.

These cells were until recently occupied by captives and a few sorry, bedraggled rangers of the Black Arrows. Now, however, they are empty, their former occupants dead and eaten.

If the PCs are having a particularly bad time retaking the fort or are severely overmatched, you can place additional surviving Black Arrows in these cells, waiting for rescue. They'll need healing and gear, but once freed are eager to aid in retaking the fort. Some might be young men-at-arms in training and rangers of the fort, who if armed, can aid the PCs. Some may even be adventurers. In a pinch, you can use the pre-generated characters presented on pages 94–95 as NPCs held captive here who can lend their aid to the party.

B37. Lizard Warrens (EL 9)

These dank caves of dirt and stone wind and bend dizzyingly, narrowing to as small as three feet wide at points. In places claws of exposed tree roots hang from the ceiling.

combat, preferring to fight with her rapier and dagger and activating *false life* on the first round of combat. If faced with overwhelming odds or brought below 80 hit points, she attempts to flee, recover, and then attack the PCs again in an area where she has more room to move around so she can utilize her spells more effectively.

Morale Lucrecia attempts to flee to the Hook Mountain clanhold if brought below 40 hit points—if she escapes, she'll be encountered at Barl Breakbones' side in area **D9**.

STATISTICS

Str 18, **Dex** 23, **Con** 20, **Int** 20, **Wis** 16, **Cha** 23

Base Atk +13; **Grp** +21

Feats Combat Expertise, Improved Feint, Improved Two-Weapon

Creatures: These winding tunnels are the nesting ground for a large pack of shocker lizards that have infested the place for decades. Introduced secretly to the caves years ago by a Black Arrow who had a soft spot for the cute little things, the lizards took to the environs with an unexpected tenacity. Since that ranger's death, the lizards have established a fairly stable ecosystem here, feeding happily on the grubs, cockroaches, and centipedes that scuttle around the caves. The fact that their presence keeps these vermin from infesting the keep above was enough (barely) for the rest of the Black Arrows to leave the lizards be, but during shocker lizard mating season the rangers took care to light stacks of bitterbark wood chips (the scent of which the lizards find repugnant) to keep them from swarming up into the castle.

The shocker lizards are relatively nonagressive as long as intruders move slowly through the warrens, don't approach too closely to any of the several egg mounds in the caves, and don't hurt the lizards. If any of these conditions are broken, the dozen adult lizards in the warrens quickly rise to the defense of their home.

SHOCKER LIZARDS (12)   **CR 2**
hp 13 each (MM 224)

Rannick Reclaimed

With the ogres slaughtered to the last or driven back up the mountainside, the PCs liberate Fort Rannick. Yet the Order of the Black Arrows remains dead; Vale and Jarkardros alone cannot carry the torch, and both have their own reasons for not wishing to remain in the region. Fort Rannick is reclaimed, but it is without a master.

Although Fort Rannick was built by funds from Magnimar over four decades ago, it's been under the jurisdiction of Turtleback Ferry for most of that time. When Mayor Maelin Shreed learns of the fate of the Black Arrows and that the PCs have defeated the ogres who claimed the keep, he is quite impressed and is quick to offer stewardship of Fort Rannick to the PCs in thanks and reward. Of course, maintaining a keep at the edge of civilization might in some ways be more than the PCs bargain for.

The rest of this adventure makes no assumptions about how the PCs decide to handle their new roles as lords and ladies of Varisia. Beyond this adventure, Fort Rannick can still serve the PCs as a handy base for their operations in Varisia, if only due to its centralized location. If they do decide to take on the mantle of Lords of Rannick, consult "Keeping the Keep" on page 54 of this volume for some tips, background on maintaining castles, and several adventure ideas that can spring from the roles the PCs have found themselves in.

PART THREE: DOWN COMES THE RAIN

Winter rises, but before her cold breath descends on the Hook, the skies darken like blood-muddied water, and ominous clouds writhe on the horizon, bringing the near-constant rain to new heights of torrential downpours. Storms go on for days without the sun so much as peeking from behind her cloudy veil, and the rivers and lakes begin to swell. Pure misery reigns as cold and wet become the order of every day, and mud seems to befoul every square foot of the region.

These unnatural rains are all part of the evil design Mokmurian's minions have for the region. Barl Breakbones' primary goal on Hook Mountain is to push the Kreeg ogres to forge weapons for the army gathering on the Storval Plateau, and then to personally lead the ogres up to join that army. The destruction of Fort Rannick was merely an idle diversion for the stone giant. Less of a diversion are the plans Lucrecia has for Turtleback Ferry. With the aid of a covey of annis hags allied with the Kreegs, Barl and Lucrecia hit upon the plan to mark as many of the residents of Turtleback Ferry for Karzoug's *runewell* as possible and then flood the village, killing hundreds and giving their runelord a sudden and unexpected boost of soul energy. To engineer the flood, Barl sent a group of ogres to Skull's Crossing, the immense dam that holds back the waters of the Storval Deep, with orders to begin weakening the structure. At the same time, the necromancer giant has employed a covey of hags to use their *control weather* ability to ensure constant rain in the region so that the waters near the Storval side of the dam are properly swollen. The combination, he hopes, should soon result in a catastrophic flood. Of course, two factors Barl wasn't counting on were the PCs and a tribe of trolls who dwell in Skull's Crossing and didn't take lightly to ogres coming to break down their home.

A few days after the PCs reclaim Fort Rannick, a third factor emerges. As the ogres work at the dam, hammering at it with their picks and hooks, the rhythmic sounds sing through the massive stones of the dam and into the waters of the Storval Deep, where one of the lake's most notorious denizens takes notice. This is the monster Black Magga, and on this day, she arrives at the dam to investigate the strange sounds. Finding several ogres hacking away at the stone near the dam's eastern side, she attacks, eager to taste these large juicy-looking morsels. As she surges up onto the dam to do so, her bulk proves the final straw and the ogre-weakened section collapses. Black Magga, several ogres, and hundreds of tons of stone fall down along the face into the valley below, followed by a deluge of water. It doesn't take long for the flood to reach Turtleback Ferry.

By now, the villagers know the heroes not only laid low "those damnable Grauls," but also liberated and reclaimed Fort Rannick. When the flood strikes, people begin evacuating at once, but the waters rise rapidly. Soon after the flooding begins, a villager (a hunter named Bran Fered) rides hellbent up the road north as the banks of the Skull River rise ever higher, threatening to swamp the road and bridge in hours. His report to the PCs is panicked and breathless.

"They are drowning, my lords! The Skull surges along its banks. Even the waters of Claybottom invade the shore and spill across the land. Turtleback Ferry will be gone by morning! The people are doing their best to evacuate, but many are trapped in their attics watching the floodwaters rise. Father Shreed is holed up in the cathedral with the sick, and they can't be moved easily, and what's worse, that old church could collapse any minute. You must help us!"

There should be little time to prepare. Press upon the PCs that if they do not depart immediately, they stand little chance of saving the citizens of Turtleback Ferry. Unless the PCs can all fly, they must hurry if they wish to use the road to reach Turtleback Ferry, for it would seem that the floodwaters of the rising Skull River will swamp it within hours. In fact, the flooding won't reach the point where the roads are washed away quite yet (the damage Black Magga did to the dam wasn't quite that extensive), but it should spur the PCs on nonetheless. As long as they make haste, they should reach Turtleback Ferry in time to help. When the PCs arrive on the scene, read them the following:

The village of Turtleback Ferry is drowning. The muddy, surging waters of the Skull River tear through the center of the community to fill Claybottom Lake with a terrible fury—many of the buildings that once sat comfortable on the river's banks are already flooding and in danger of collapsing from the rushing water. A group of children and a woman huddle aboard one of the old turtleshell ferryboats, the tiny flood-bashed vessel lodged up against the general store and threatening to capsize at any moment. Beyond, the town's church stands solid, its foundations already three feet deep in floodwaters. Frantic movement is visible in the upstairs windows as townsfolk trapped inside rush about in a desperate attempt to save scriptures, comfort the sick, and pray for deliverance.

Saving the School Children (EL 5)

When the flash flood struck, Tillia Henkenson was instructing a class of young boys and girls in the schoolhouse. As the floodwaters poured into the front door of the riverfront building, they evacuated and sought out one of the ferries for shelter, but were then pinned to the side of the general store by the rushing water before they could clamber to safety on the other side. They have languished here for the past several hours, watching the waters rise. And as the PCs arrive, a new threat makes itself clear.

Creature: The villagers are not the only ones being uprooted by the flood. A 24-foot-long nightbelly boa constrictor, one of the more dangerous predators to ply the river, was dislodged by the waters several miles upstream and has been carried by the current all the way to the village. As the PCs attempt to mount a rescue, the waters carry the snake up against the side of the ferry. The constrictor rises from the water with a loud hiss and attacks, attempting to constrict and swallow young Tabitha Kramm, pigtails, freckles, and all. Tillia Henkenson screams along with the rest of the children, powerless to stop the ravenous reptile. This task falls to the PCs.

NIGHTBELLY BOA   CR 5
hp 63 (MM 280, giant constrictor snake)

Development: A DC 30 Strength check is required to pull the boat to shore using a rope. Alternately, the PCs could rescue the children themselves; it's a DC 25 Swim check to reach the ferry, which is 15 feet from shore. Flight, water walking, and teleportation make much safer methods for rescuing the children.

Ad Hoc Experience Award: If the PCs rescue the children and the schoolmarm, award them a CR 8 experience award. In addition, Tillia Henkenson gushes all over them and sends fresh-baked pies to Rannick every week thereafter in gratitude.

Black Magga Rises (EL 15)

Not long after the PCs rescue the schoolchildren, something more harrowing develops. Black Magga herself, damaged from her fall and furious at the sudden awkward turn of events, comes into town.

Give the PCs a DC 20 Spot check. Those who succeed notice what at first appears to be a huge black tree being swept downriver on a collision course with the church. Moments before the "tree" hits, it submerges. A few moments later, the floodwaters surge violently, and with a thunderous roar, Black Magga rises from the flood.

Creature: The sight of the immense monster—its primeval head rising as high as the church steeple—sends the villagers of Turtleback Ferry into a blind panic. No one even notices that the rains have stopped, and that perhaps the flood waters are already beginning to slow. For now, the spectacle of the lake monster seemingly preparing to destroy the church is all that matters.

If left to her own devices, that is precisely what Black Magga does. She takes less than five minutes to reduce the chapel to rubble, and when she's done, nothing remains—the two dozen villagers who had sought shelter within are either crushed to death or eaten by the ravenous menace.

It's unlikely that the PCs are much of a match for Black Magga, even in her current damaged state. Yet fortunately for them, they

need not slay her to drive her off. If the PCs engage the monster, she fights back for only a few rounds (see her tactics below).

BLACK MAGGA   CR 15

hp 217 (currently 152, see page 88)

TACTICS

During Combat On the first round of combat, Black Magga uses her breath of madness ability on the PCs. On the second round, she attacks the PCs, moving up to one of them to bite. On the third round, she repeats this tactic, adding her tentacles if she wasn't able to make a full attack action on round two.

Morale Black Magga retreats on the fourth round of combat, dropping any foes she's constricting, deciding that tangling with these unknown enemies is not currently in her best interest. Alternately, she retreats if the PCs bring her below 80 hit points before round four. Abandoning Turtleback Ferry and the PCs (for now), she surges downriver (possibly destroying a few minor buildings as she crashes by) and vanishes into the depths of Claybottom Lake.

Development: After Black Magga is forced to retreat, a cheer rises from the villagers who have gathered on the shores to watch. It doesn't take but a moment longer for them to notice that the floodwaters seem to be receding.

It should be obvious that the villagers' initial fear that Skull's Crossing has burst has not come to pass, yet the sudden rush of water seems to indicate something dire has happened. Several locals certainly recognize Black Magga from local legend and can explain that the monster was said to dwell in the Storval Deep, not Skull River.

All signs point north—something must have happened at Skull's Crossing. When, in the past, storms threatened to spill over the dam, the structure's floodgates opened automatically to release water pressure in a controlled flow. None in Turtleback Ferry know exactly how the mechanisim for opening the floodgates works, as Skull's Crossing has long been the den of a tribe of trolls known as the Skulltakers. Yet as long as anyone can remember, the floodgates have functioned without fault. If the floodgates are malfunctioning, someone needs to brave the wrath of the Skulltaker trolls to determine what, if anything, can be done to repair the ancient Thassilonian structure before a cataclysmic flood washes the entire region away.

Turtleback Ferry is far from a rich village, but if the PCs can prevent a more deadly flood by opening the floodgates, Mayor Shreed promises the PCs a reward of 1,000 gp. He can be talked up to as high as 2,000 gp with a DC 30 Diplomacy check.

Ad Hoc Experience Award: For driving off Black Magga, award the PCs a CR 10 experience award.

Skull's Crossing

Thassilonian monuments are a fact of life in Varisia. Most of these ancient structures are only now beginning to erode as their once-powerful wards and magical enhancements fade with the passage of millennia—yet they still bear an air of antiquity that cannot be denied. No one doubts that these monuments are from a time in the distant past, yet few comprehend that they date from over 10,000 years ago.

Skull's Crossing was one of the final—and perhaps most ambitious—projects Runelord Karzoug's giants erected. Much of the stone used to craft the Shalastian monuments scattered throughout Varisia was taken from an immense quarry in the heart of the Storval Plateau. It took centuries, but near the end, the quarry finally played out and all that remained was a vast canyon. Karzoug had little use for or interest in the ugly scar, and so ordered the construction of Skull's Crossing at its southern end to transform the quarry into the region's largest lake.

As with many of his projects that didn't feature his own countenance, the dam incorporated one of Karzoug's favorite design elements—the human skull. The colossal dam is decorated with thousands of them. Five immense skulls adorn the center of the dam's face—ancient machinery built into the dam allowed the jaws of these skulls to be opened or closed to act as floodgates should the waters of the Storval Rise ever flow too high. This machinery still functions, but the source of power, a pair of pit fiends imprisoned in life-draining magic circles, has faltered. If the PCs hope to save Turtleback Ferry, they must not only defeat the ogres bent on destroying the dam and the trolls who have claimed it as their lair—they must also find a way to power the floodgates one more time, perhaps with the aid of a dying pit fiend who has fueled Skull's Crossing for 10,000 years.

C1. Western Shore

Spanning the great breadth of the gorge is Skull's Crossing. The massive wall of stone holds back the waters of the Storval Deep—but only just. Thousands of skulls have been carved into the dam's face, while five larger ones decorate the middle length. The easternmost of these immense skulls is all but hidden by a steady flow of cascading water pouring through what appears to be a recent break in the dam. For now, the ancient dam seems to be holding its own against the Storval Deep, but unless these rains end soon the recent flood looks to be but a minor precursor to a fantastic disaster.

The eastern slopes of the gorge are sheer and slick with rain, but to the west, a narrow stone stairway, its edge decorated with hundreds of poles bearing the skulls of as many different creatures, winds up to a cave mouth near the western rim of the dam itself.

The break in the dam was where Black Magga attacked the ogres and inadvertently finished the job that they started. Since then, the ogres have relocated to the other side of the dam at area **C6** to continue their work. The rain starts again not long after the PCs arrive here, but before it does, a DC 20 Spot check is enough for them to notice several lumbering shapes moving about on the dam's upper reach at this point.

C2. The Stairway of Skulls

A seven-foot-wide winding stairway of stone climbs the cliff face here, reaching a height of nearly two hundred feet before ending at a cave mouth above. Hundreds of stakes line the edges of the stairway, many of them decorated with skulls—some animal, some humanoid, all marked with a strange skull-shaped rune on the brow.

Anyone who speaks Giant recognizes the runes on the skulls as warnings—these are territory markers for the Skulltaker trolls that dwell in the region. The stairs themselves are sized for Large creatures, and as such require a DC 7 Climb check for Medium or smaller folk to ascend. A fall results in a plummet of 1d10×10 feet before the victim reaches one of the many narrow ledges that line the cliff face.

C3. Ettin's Doorstep

The short passageway ends here, but to the west, a fifteen-foot-high ledge provides access to a cave beyond.

It's a DC 15 Climb check to scramble up the ledge, since the surface is so crumbly. Worse, the crumbling pebbles impart a −4 penalty on Move Silently checks—Gorger and Chaw is likely to hear anyone trying to get into his home via this route.

C4. Gorger and Chaw's Lair (EL 6)

The air in this forty-foot-high cave is thankfully fresh as a brisk breeze whistles through from the north, yet still, the dozens of mostly eaten firepelt cougars, deer, and even a few humans heaped along the walls fill the room with a stomach-turning stink.

Creature: This cave has long been the lair of an ettin named Gorger and Chaw. When the Skulltaker trolls moved into the region, they formed an alliance with the ettin—as long as he left the dam itself to the trolls and served as a guard for this approach to its heights, he would be allowed to remain in the region. Gorger and Chaw saw no problem with this arrangement, since there's nothing to interest him on the dam anyway. Ever since, he's been regarded as an honorary member of the tribe.

When the ogres arrived, Gorger and Chaw was initially inclined to kill them, but when the ogres offered the ettin a hefty bribe of several delicious smoked humans, Gorger and Chaw decided to look the other way. Now, the ettin is wracked with guilt about failing the Skulltaker tribe, and is afraid to head up to the dam to help them fight the ogres for fear that the trolls will smell his treachery. He sees the PCs as an opportunity to prove his loyalty to the tribe, and attacks them on sight with the battle cry "YOU NO BRIBE ME! I SMASH YOU FOR SKULLTAKERS!"

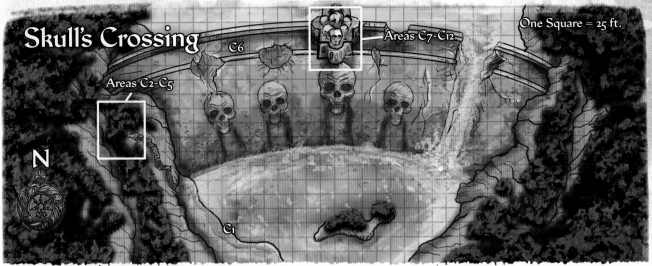

Skull's Crossing

One Square = 25 ft.

Areas C7-C12

C6

Areas C2-C5

N

C1

Western Caves

One Square = 5 ft.

C5

C4

C3

C2

Skull's Watch

One Square = 5 ft.

C7

C8

C9

C11

C12

C10

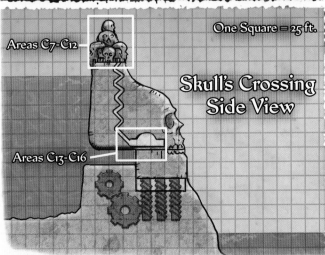

Areas C7-C12

Skull's Crossing Side View

One Square = 25 ft.

Areas C13-C16

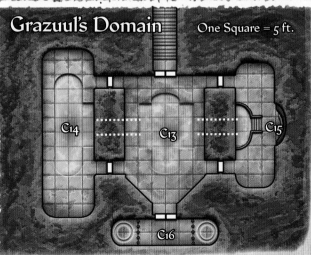

Grazuul's Domain

One Square = 5 ft.

C14

C13

C15

C16

GORGER AND CHAW   CR 6
Ettin
hp 65 (MM 106)

Treasure: Gorger and Chaw has collected a fair bit of treasure over the years. The ettin keeps this treasure in a disorganized heap near his collection of sleeping furs in the northeastern cave. The loot consists of 693 gp, 1,240 sp, a velvet pouch containing six 100 gp pearls, a *phylactery of undead turning*, and an ivory scroll tube inset with strips of jade (itself worth 300 gp) that contains a scroll of *cone of cold, hold monster,* and *telekinesis.*

C5. Upper Passage

As with the one in area **C3**, this fifteen-foot-high ledge requires a DC 15 Climb check to scale. The stairs above lead up to the top of the dam itself.

C6. Ogre Demolition Crew (EL 7)

The upper walk of Skull's Crossing is relatively clear of rubble, though a three-inch layer of water has pooled across much of its surface. Here and there, sections of the dam's surface have crumbled away, although this damage appears relatively old. A tower of skull-shaped domes sits at the center of the dam's walk. To the north surge the choppy waters of the Storval Deep, while to the south, the slope of the dam's face drops away to a muddy lake nearly three hundred feet below.

Anyone who walks along the dam's edge must make a DC 12 Balance check, as the rock along the edges is particularly slippery with algae and water. A fall off the north side results in a short drop into the stormy water—fallers take no damage, but it's a DC 15 Swim check to stay afloat. A fall off the south side is a rough tumble down the steeply sloped surface into the water below for 20d6 points of damage.

Creatures: Sent by Barl Breakbones himself, the team of ogre demolitionists charged with weakening Skull's Crossing originally numbered two dozen. After several fights with the Skulltaker trolls and the disaster to the east when Black Magga attacked, this group is down to only four miserable, tired, and sick ogres led by a barbarian named Malugus. Jaagrath's third son, Malugus initially viewed the task of destroying Skull's Crossing as a tremendous honor, but now he's close to giving up on the entire thing and fleeing east into the Wyvern Mountains. Malugus and his ogres have just recently reached this side of the dam after fighting their way through area **C7**, and while he takes a nice long break, sitting on a block of stone in the rain, he's put his four remaining henchogres to work hammering their hooks against the stone.

All five ogres are exhausted from the work and conditions. They move at half speed and have a –6 penalty to Strength and Dexterity. Malugus has already used both of his rages for the day. The EL for this encounter is reduced slightly to account for the ogres' exhaustion.

MALUGUS KREEG   CR 7
Male ogre barbarian 4
hp 79 (MM 199)

EXHAUSTED OGRES (4)   CR 3
Male ogre barbarian 4
hp 29 each (MM 199)

Skull's Watch (Areas C7–C12)

The two northern double doors that lead into this structure have been repeatedly smashed by the ogres, only to be hastily repaired by the Skulltaker trolls that dwell inside. They no longer open, and must be pushed down with a DC 24 Strength check to access area **C7**. The two southern doors are intact and barred from the inside—they can be forced open with a DC 28 Strength check. The "windows" into the structure are in fact the eye sockets of the skull-shaped facade; they're five feet in diameter and 10 feet off the ground. It's a DC 10 Climb check to scramble up to one of them, but entry through any of these windows is perhaps the simplest way into Skull's Watch.

C7. Battlefield (EL 9)

Piles of rubble dominate this large room, along with bits of flesh, broken weapons, splashes of blood, and a few dead ogres that have been torn limb from limb. Wind and rain howls through circular openings to the north that look out over the Storval Deep, and puddles of water have collected on the floor. Thick sheets of ropy green fungus grow along the walls here, winding in through both the windows and through numerous cracks in the domed ceiling thirty feet above; behind the fungal vines, the walls are decorated with hundreds of skull-shaped carvings.

Creatures: Although the trolls recover quickly from the ogre attacks, several of them perished when the ogres hit on the idea of throwing trolls over the edge of the dam once they were beaten unconscious in battle, drowning the trolls before they regenerated back to consciousness. All that remain now are four trolls. They've taken the time to hide among the fungus hanging down along the walls, and while they're expecting ogres, they react to the PCs' intrusion with the same anger and shrieking wrath.

TROLLS (4)   CR 5
hp 63 each (MM 247)

C8–C9. Skulltaker Dens

The walls of this room are thick with strange green ropy fungus that hangs down over several windows, almost like curtains. Several large nests made of the stuff cover the floor.

These rooms were used by the Skulltakers as lairs, but now that so few remain alive, they've been all but abandoned.

Treasure: A DC 25 Search of area **C9** uncovers a loose stone near the base of the southern wall that hides a small cache of treasure one of the trolls hid from his kin. The cache consists of a cracked emerald worth 400 gp, a bent gold comb that looks like a behir (with its legs comprising the comb's teeth) with tiny pearls for eyes worth 850 gp, and a pair of lacy pink *gloves of arrow snaring* that were too small and effeminate for the troll to wear (but since they never grow dirty and always smell faintly of lilacs, the troll was strangely intrigued by them).

C10. Observation Deck

Three round windows in this room look out over the southern view from Skull's Crossing. Additional skull carvings decorate the walls, ceiling, and even the floor. In the middle of the north wall stand massive stone double doors, their smooth surfaces smeared with graffiti written in dried blood.

Though unlocked, the double doors are exceptionally heavy, and their hinges are old and gritty. A DC 22 Strength check is required to open them. The graffiti, written by the trolls in Giant, reads: "BELOW DWELLS WET PAPA GRAZUUL! ALL HAIL WET PAPA GRAZUUL!"

Beyond the doors, a flight of stone steps leads down into the darkness, descending 150 feet to area **C13**.

C11. Storeroom

This room is nearly clogged with thick coils of the strange vine-like fungal growths, transforming the chamber into a miniature jungle that reeks of damp mold.

Although all of this fungus is harmless, the thickness with which the stuff grows in here may intrigue the PCs. The reason behind the thick growths is mundane—the trolls simply never used this room and never cleared the stuff out.

C12. Collapsed Room

The southwestern section of this ancient room has collapsed away, leaving a treacherous-looking gap in the wall overlooking the lower lake far below.

Although the collapse looks dangerous, the room itself remains stable. This unofficial entrance to Skull's Watch could be used by flying PCs to avoid encounters with the trolls to the north.

C13. Observation Pool (EL 10)

This cold, damp room features a large pool in the floor, the edges of which are caked with pale yellow slime and fungus. The surface of the pool bears a similar film. Additional carvings of skulls decorate the walls here. To the south, an impressive mound of skulls—mostly from humanoids—lies heaped against the wall, where they partially block a large stone double door.

The film of algae on top of the pool of water is foul-smelling but harmless. The pool itself is 15 feet deep. Submerged tunnels connect the bottom of this pool to the ones in areas **C14** and **C15**.

The mound of hundreds of skulls to the south must be cleared away (a task that would take one person 10 minutes to accomplish) before the door to area **C16** can be opened.

Creatures: This room is the lair of the Skulltaker chieftain, an aquatic troll named Grazuul. Hardly more intelligent than an animal, Grazuul barely comprehends that the "dry ones" who live above think of him as their lord—all he knows is that he appreciates their regular offerings of skulls. Grazuul particularly enjoys the look and feel of a freshly polished skull, which is why he's lived most of his life deep inside of Skull's Crossing. One of his favorite pastimes, in fact, is to tear away the flesh of his own face so he can feel the cool water rushing against the raw bone of his own skull before the flesh regenerates back.

Grazuul's explorations of the drowned caverns and mines at the bottom of the Storval Deep have turned up all manner of strange and ancient treasures that have been forgotten since the fall of Thassilon. One such item is the magical adamantine military fork he carries. While this pole arm is sized for a Medium foe (same statistics as a ranseur), and is somewhat awkward for the scrag to use, he still enjoys the ease with which the weapon's tines punch through anything with ease, be it flesh, wood, stone, or metal.

GRAZUUL   CR 10

Male scrag fighter 5

CE Large giant

Init +4; **Senses** darkvision 90 ft., low-light vision, scent; Listen +4,
Spot +5

DEFENSE

AC 19, touch 13, flat-footed 15
(+4 Dex, +6 natural, –1 size)

hp 140 (6d8+5d10+77); regeneration 5 (acid and fire)

Fort +16, **Ref** +7, **Will** +3

OFFENSE

Spd 20 ft., swim 40 ft.

Melee Medium +1 vicious adamantine military fork +16/+11
(2d4+14/×3 plus 2d6) and
bite +15 (1d6+4) or
2 claws +18 (1d6+11/19–20) and
bite +15 (1d6+4)

Space 10 ft.; **Reach** 10 ft.

Special Attacks rend 2d6+13

TACTICS

During Combat Grazuul attempts to remain in the water
throughout the entire combat so he can continue enjoying the
effects of his regeneration, but once he's brought below 50 hit
points, he drops his military fork and switches over to using his
claws to let his regeneration catch up with all the damage he'd
been doing to himself by using the vicious weapon. If facing
characters wearing heavy armor, he clambers out of his
pool to try to bull rush them into the water if the
opportunity presents itself.

Morale Grazuul fights to the death, confident that his
regeneration will save him if he's defeated. If, on the
other hand, the PCs bring a lot of fire and acid against
him, he abandons
Skull's Crossing
entirely once
brought below 20
hit points and flees into area
C14 and thence north into the Storval Deep.

STATISTICS

Str 28, **Dex** 18, **Con** 24, **Int** 4, **Wis** 11,
Cha 8

Base Atk +9; **Grp** +22

Feats Combat Reflexes, Improved Bull
Rush, Improved Critical (claw),
Multiattack, Power Attack, Weapon

Focus (claw), Weapon Specialization (claw)

Skills Listen +4, Spot +5, Swim +22

Languages Giant

Gear Medium +1 vicious adamantine military fork

C14. Flood Chamber Access

This narrow chamber is empty save for a long, ten-foot-wide pool.

The pool in this room is 15 feet deep. A submerged tunnel
connects it to area **C13**. In the bottom of the pool (just under
the "**C14**" tag) is a secret door (Search DC 20 to locate) that, if
opened, leads through a series of several doors that can only be
opened one at a time, and eventually to the underwater channel
leading to the floodway to the Storval Deep. It was through this
route that Grazuul came to these chambers years ago.

C15. Floodgate Controls

A pool of water sits against the wall to the west of this chamber,
with a set of steps leading down into it along the pool's east side.
Opposite the steps is an alcove in which rises a fantastically detailed
scale model of Skull's Crossing. The five skulls along its face seem
to be actual human skulls, the bone polished to a gleeming sheen.

GRAZUUL

This scale model of Skull's Crossing once served to help regulate the water level on the Storval Deep side of the dam. When the water rose to within 30 feet of the top of the dam, this device would automatically open the five floodgates to prevent a catastrophic failure. The floodgates themselves were powered by the lifeforce of the two pit fiends once trapped in area **C16**, but now that one of them is dead and the other is nearly so, not enough power remains to operate this failsafe. An examination of the skulls reveals that the jaws of each can be pulled down like levers to reveal tubes leading into the wall. The scale model itself radiates strong transmutation magic.

C16. Infernal Engines

This narrow chamber ends at a curved alcove to the east and west. Each alcove is enclosed by a dull iron portcullis. A nearby winch next to each provides a way to raise or lower the gates. Beyond each portcullis a circle of runes glows with a faint orange light on the floor. Inside the circle to the west is a pile of crimson ash, while inside the circle to the east is curled what appears to be a long-dead devil, its flesh taut and dry on its bones.

These two magic circles are powerful prisons that once held the energy source for Skull's Crossing's floodgates—a pair of pit fiends Karzoug captured. Whenever the floodgates needed to be opened, the magic circles drained life energy (inflicting a negative level upon the pit fiend trapped inside) and used it to power the immense gears hidden deep within the dam that governed the use of the floodgates. Over the 10,000 years, powerful storms caused the Storval Deep to rise to flood levels only 150 times. For most of those occurences, the trapped pit fiends recovered from the energy drain, but as the years wore on, they began failing their saving throws to shrug off the negative levels and grew progressively weaker. When the last powerful storm wracked the region and triggered the dam's flood controls 54 years ago, one of the two pit fiends died, and its body crumbled to crimson ash. Today, there is simply not enough lifeforce remaining to power the floodgates, and unless this changes soon, the Storval Deep will rise above the dam's level and flood the lands to the south.

The "dead" pit fiend in the eastern magic circle is not actually dead—it can be recognized as a pit fiend with a DC 30 Knowledge (the planes) check. Once a powerful devil named Avaxial, the pit fiend has been drained down to 1 Hit Die. His body now feeble, the devil has spent the last several decades in a comatose fugue, barely able to move. When the PCs enter this area, Avaxial rouses from his torpor to feebly reach for one of them, gasping in a raw whisper for freedom. As long as the pit fiend remains trapped in the magic circle, he can use neither his supernatural abilities nor his spell-like abilities, but he can still communicate. He begs the PCs to dispel the magic of the circle that traps him, or barring that, to destroy the runes so he may escape. The circle itself functions at caster level 20th, and if a *dispel magic* successfully affects it, the circle is only rendered nonmagical for 1d4 rounds—long enough for the pit fiend to use *greater teleport* to flee to a distant sanctuary to begin the long process of recovering from his 10,000 year ordeal. Destroying the circle is even more difficult, for the runes themselves are set in a ring of magical stone that must be physically destroyed by weapons or magic to render the circle inert.

Wise PCs might take advantage of the pit fiend's plight to learn how to open the floodgates. Avaxial tries to bargain with the PCs, hoping to extract promises of release in exchange for what he knows, but he lacks the will and energy to press the deal too far. Over the millennia, the devil has gone somewhat insane. He knows nothing of Thassilon (as he was conjured into this trap from the Hells itself) and remembers his captor only as a vague hatred and a name—Karzoug. Avaxial does know he's been used for the past age as an engine to power the floodgates—he can sense the shape of the dam around him and can feel the gates open. He knows that the gates open automatically when the waters rise high enough, and can even feel those waters rising. He's felt the circle tugging at the last shards of his spirit for days, if not weeks now, but knows that since his one-time companion succumbed over five decades ago, there's simply not enough life left to activate the floodgates.

Skull's Crossing requires only one level of energy in the west circle to trigger the floodgates. Both magic circles function as cages only for those they were designed to constrain—anyone else can step into and out of either circle with ease. As soon as a living creature is within each circle, though, the dam awakens with a rumble. Both creatures in each circle gain a negative level as the floodgates in the dam grind open, releasing waters from the Storval Deep in a constrained torrent into the valley below. It's a DC 20 Fortitude save to remove one of these negative levels. Back at Turtleback Ferry, the waters rise again, but this time the rise is more controlled and less destructive—the peril of the storms is averted.

Any creature (including summoned creatures) with only 1 Hit Die that gains a negative level from one of these circles is immediately reduced to ashes—if a creature steps into the west circle before Avaxial is released from his own circle, this is his fate. The moral repurcussions of destroying a pit fiend in this manner are left for philosophers to argue, but the act certainly fufills the greater good of saving Turtleback Ferry.

No stat block is given for Avaxial, as the devil is in no condition to fight or defend himself.

MAGIC CIRCLE

hp 120; **Hardness** 16; **Break DC** 34

Development: If the PCs fail to open the floodgates and relieve the pressure building on Skull's Crossing, the dam is fated to burst only 1d4 days after this failure. This may be enough time to evacuate Turtleback Ferry, but the village itself is doomed to destruction when a surge of water washes down from the mountains.

Ad Hoc Experience Award: If the PCs open the floodgates, award them a CR 10 experience award.

PART FOUR: THE HAUNTED HEART

Once the PCs have reclaimed Fort Rannick and saved Turtleback Ferry from the flood, all that remains for them to do is to confront Barl Breakbones and defeat the remaining Kreegs in their lair high up on the face of Hook Mountain. Yet this final step might not be obvious. Certainly, if the PCs have vengeance in their hearts, they may seek out the Kreeg hold on their own. If they need further encouragement to seek out Barl Breakbones, though, you can use this part to give them a reason to climb Hook Mountain.

The Shimmerglens have long been shrouded in mystery, for these trackless swamps are said to lie quite close to the First World of the Fey, particularly where they border Sanos Forest. Capricious and sometimes malicious creatures are known to harass travelers in this domain. The Wicker Walk between Sanos Forest and the hamlet of Bitter Hollow was built expressly to offer travelers a way to cross through the swamps without annoying the area's denizens, but stories still abound of nixies laying traps to confuse and baffle travelers, of nymphs seducing men and women and leaving them besotted and lost in the marsh, or of sprites stealing supplies and replacing them with rotten fish, poison mushrooms, or disturbing little dolls made of clay and string.

But now, a darker horror holds court in the heart of the riverside swampland. A nymph named Myriana, once a princess of the Shimmerglens and the lover of Fort Rannick's former commander, has been brutally murdered. Her spirit returned to her home in the swamps, and now her entire domain has become polluted with her restless hate. And the focus of this misplaced hate is those whom she once counted as her court.

Something evil has appeared in a section of the Shimmerglens known as Whitewillow. Trappers and hunters traditionally only ply their trade along the shores of the Shimmerglens, and avoid going beyond sight of Claybottom Lake, for beyond this border the fey rule. Yet recently, encounters with nixies, sprites, and other strange creatures have increased along this border, almost as if something deeper in the swamp were pushing them outward.

A Desperate Plea

The PCs get their first glimpse of the secret relationship between Lamatar and Myriana if they find the hidden compartment in the commander's quarters of Fort Rannick (area **B30**). If they don't find this cache, you should endeavor to let them (or an assistant) discover it at some point after they've defeated the Kreegs occupying the fort and are going about the business of repairing the castle and making it their new home, so that when they receive a visit from one of Myriana's desperate allies, they won't be caught completely off guard.

When the Kreegs attacked Fort Rannick, Lamatar doomed his lover by casting an *animal messenger* spell and sending the animal out to deliver the grim news that the fort was under attack, hoping that she would shore up her own defenses around Whitewillow in the event that the ogres were planning assaults

further south. Of course, Myriana immediately made her way north to do what she could to help her lover, but she arrived too late. She caught up with the Kreegs halfway up Hook Mountain, and although she managed to kill nearly half of the ogres in her attempt to free Lamatar, she was eventually overpowered and torn limb from limb before her lover's despairing eyes. Her spirit, anguished and insane, returned to her realm in the Shimmerglens where she became a ghost, and now her madness has twisted and corrupted Whitewillow into a place of growing evil. Many of her servants and minions have perished or become corrupted as well, but one loyal pixie, a normally chattery fellow named Yap, avoided this fate by fleeing into the Land of Big Folk.

It takes Yap several weeks, but eventually he learns where Myriana's lover used to live. Hoping to find Lamatar, or help of any sort, he makes his way north and eventually arrives at Fort Rannick. (If the PCs are no longer there, he finds out they cleared out the ogres and seeks them out wherever they might have gone.) Regardless of whom the nervous pixie first contacts, he's quickly diverted to the PCs as the current lords of the fort. Yap looks like a typical pixie—a waifishly thin humanoid with gossamer wings, large expressive eyes, long pointed ears, and a diminutive two-foot-tall stature. His rumpled clothes and eyes puffy from crying, though, indicate just how much things are out of place for the poor creature. Once Yap has the PCs' attention, he delivers his message and plea in a rapid, breathless speech, as if he's afraid at any moment the PCs will turn him away.

"My mistress, she is… ill. Very ill. Death would have been a kindness. The land sickens with her heart, and it cannot be cleansed until her misery is purged. I cannot do this myself. Please, you must help her! You are friends with her human lover, yes? He wouldn't leave her like this! I can take you to her—maybe you can do something. I have tried everything to cure her forlorn heart, but to no avail. She wails and moans in Whitewillow, and the trees and plants and nixies and frogs and *everything* are dying or worse! I can take you there! *Please!*"

Yap doesn't know that Lamatar is dead, and if the PCs tell him, he breaks down in a fit of mournful cries. Only a DC 30 Diplomacy check or a promise that they'll help him mend his lady's broken heart quiets him.

Assuming the PCs agree to aid Yap, the pixie's mood brightens considerably as hope returns. He wants to leave immediately, but agrees to wait for the PCs to prepare for the journey if they need to. The Shimmerglens themselves quickly grow tangled and densely packed once one travels out of sight of the swamp's edge—the easiest way to get around is by rowboat, navigating via the narrow channels of water. The *boots of the mire* from Lamatar's hidden cache would certainly help one of the PCs, in any event. This far from the mountains, the hag covey's *control weather* spells are far enough removed that the rains that have been plaguing the northern areas are thankfully absent—all that remains is the subtle chill of winter's approach. As the PCs delve deeper into the swamp, feel free to liven up their journey with encounters (using the wandering monster chart for Varisia's swamps on page 71), but with Yap's guidance, it shouldn't be long before they reach the blighted area known as Whitewillow.

YAP   CR 4

Male pixie

hp 3 (MM 236)

Whitewillow

Twisted black trees rise wretchedly from shallow pools, seeming to have lurched from the land, their arthritic branches curled into miserable tortured claws. The sun seems to scorn this place, and a cold dark mist looms within the canopy of bone-bare branches above. Evil murmurs ride an unnatural wind that flows forth from the glens, and shadows dance in the dark mists within.

The trees of Whitewillow, once beautiful and mystic with drooping boughs of sparkling ivory leaves, have gone dark and twisted with Myriana's torment. Now, they shift and move when they should not. Shadows play cruel tricks on the sharpest eyes, and sanity-shredding whispers cause even the canniest woodsman to lose his way. As Yap leads the PCs deeper into the depths of Whitewillow, the degree of the corruption grows. Spiders, fat and languid on poison, hang from trees. Dying birds twitch in the shallows. Slithering things with too many eyes squirt away through the water. Whitewillow is about a mile in diameter, and as the PCs march deeper and deeper into Myriana's madness, you can use some of the following mood-setting encounters to amplify the PCs' fears.

Apparitions of Death: Nothing but chill silence surrounds the PCs, though they occasionally glimpse tall, dark-robed figures in their peripheral vision. The creatures' enlarged skeletal claws extend from their outstretched arms as if reaching toward the party. When the PCs look, they see these apparitions are nothing more than horribly twisted black trees. If attacked, the trees weep blood and seem to cackle in the wind.

Dead Pool: A natural pool of water created by runoff from the hulking dark trees stands in a clearing ahead of the party. The water looks clear and refreshing enough, though a DC 20 Survival check notes that no algae or larval insects dwell in the pool, possibly indicating the water is poisoned. Anyone who gazes into the water too intently must make a DC 15 Will save. Failure indicates their own reflection is normal, but other party members appear reflected as decaying corpses. In addition, the other party members appear to be glaring hungrily at the PC gazing into the water as if they are about to attack and devour them. The PC immediately takes 1d4 Wisdom damage.

Ghostly Revels: All around the PCs, ghostly translucent forms emerge from the trees. Fey of all sorts—spectral satyrs, ghostly grigs, phantom nixies, and sprightly spirits float gently from the swamp around the party, followed by a parade of phantom animals. These were once the proud denizens of Whitewillow, now polluted by their mistress's unsettled soul. The fey cavort and frolic as they march, eventually washing over the PCs. They caress, dance through, and embrace the

PCs before passing. The PCs must make a DC 15 Will save or be caught in a ghostly party's path, riveted by the otherworldly spectacle. Affected creatures take 2d6 points of negative energy damage as the unnatural chill of the spectral fey burns them. The ghostly fey and their undead animals ignore the party; the unfathomable business of the dead draws them elsewhere in short order.

Mysterious Derelict: Deep in the swamp the PCs suddenly come upon a derelict ship inexplicably located hundreds of miles from the Varisian shore. The vessel is badly worn and covered in thick dark green moss, but is completely intact. The ship is deserted, but in his quarters below deck, the long-dead captain sits at a moldering darkwood harpsichord carved with demons battling angels. Still dressed in his rotten uniform, he clutches in one hand nautical charts that seem completely alien even to the most well-traveled PC, and a silver goblet inlaid with opals worth 100 gp in the other. A book of sheet music bearing several lyrical masterpieces never before heard by any of the PCs sits on the harpsichord. The songs contained in the book appear worthless unless a PC succeeds on a DC 20 Perform (any musical instrument or sing) check. The book and the wondrous music contained within are worth 5,000 gp to a collector, musician, or noble. When the PCs emerge from the ship, a white dog sits on deck watching them with milky blind eyes. The dog stares but does nothing else, eventually wandering off into the swamp and leaving behind no trace it was ever actually there.

Heart of Sadness (EL 10)

Eventually, the tangled swamp gives way to a relatively large clearing, a calm pool of unnaturally still water ringed by twisted, decayed willow trees. Wind blows, but the trees do not sway. It is as if the very land has died. Yap quails at the edge of the clearing, quietly informing the PCs, "We're here... my lady waits for you within. I dare not go any closer..." The terrified pixie steps back,

then cowers behind a gnarled tree and waits for the PCs to step into Myriana's glade.

Creature: Once soul-shakingly beautiful, the nymph princess Myriana is now a haggard, ghostly horror. Her disembodied arms float at her sides, exposed bone and sinew stretching toward her torso but ever too far out of reach. Her lower torso fades away to smoke, savaged too cruelly by the ogres for even her insane ghost to keep. But her most terrifying feature are her eyes: wells of hellish horror, crying out silently in an agony beyond anything a mortal creature could ever know. They reduce those who try to hold her gaze to gibbering children. She is beauty undone, and torment incarnate.

As the PCs enter her twisted glade, the ghostly nymph rises with a howl from the waters. Although she doesn't immediately attack the PCs, her blinding beauty is in full effect. In a shrieking, hate-filled voice, she accuses the PCs of failing Lamatar, of failing to protect Fort Rannick, and of allowing the Kreeg ogres to take him to their lair high on Hook Mountain. Yet she does not immediately attack the PCs. She allows them a few minutes to state their case, and to explain why they have come to Whitewillow. If the PCs ask her what they can do to help, she simply bemoans the fact that she has no part of her lover's body to return to life. All she asks for is a fragment, a single finger, a lock of hair—anything. Climb Hook Mountain, avenge his death, and return to her with a relic from her lover's

body—she shall take care of the rest. Unless the PCs agree to do this for her, the mournful undead loses patience soon enough and flies into a frenzy.

MYRIANA   CR 10

Female advanced nymph ghost (MM 117, 197)

CN Medium undead (augmented fey, incorporeal)

Init +5; **Senses** darkvision 60 ft., low-light vision; Listen +28, Spot +28

Aura blinding beauty (blindness, 30 ft., DC 27); corrupting gaze (2d10 damage plus 1d4 Cha damage, 30 feet, DC 25)

DEFENSE

AC 24, touch 24, flat-footed 19
   (+9 deflection, +5 Dex)

hp 78 (12d12)

Fort +13, **Ref** +22, **Will** +22

Defensive Abilities +4 turn resistance, incorporeal traits, undead traits
---
OFFENSE

Spd fly 30 ft. (perfect)

Melee draining touch +11 (1d4 Charisma drain)

Special Attacks manifestation, stunning glance (DC 25), telekinesis

Spell-Like Abilities (CL 7th)
   1/day—*dimension door*

Spells Prepared (CL 7th)
   4th—*flame strike* (DC 21), *reincarnate*
   3rd—*call lightning* (DC 20), *dominate animal* (DC 18), *summon*

nature's ally III

2nd—*chill metal* (DC 17), *flame blade*, *flaming sphere* (DC 19), *gust of wind* (DC 19)

1st—*charm animal* (DC 16), *entangle* (DC 16), *obscuring mist*, *produce flame*, *speak with animals*, *summon nature's ally I*

0—*detect magic*, *flare* (2, DC 17), *guidance*, *light*, *mending*

TACTICS

During Combat Although Myriana is undead, she was made so by despair and anguish, not hate. She would prefer to recruit the PCs rather than harm them, and fights only to defend herself. She prefers to use her stunning gaze to defeat foes without causing lasting harm, but if pressed uses her magic and corrupting gaze to get her point across.

Morale As long as her lover's body remains atop Hook Mountain, Myriana cannot be slain forever. She fights until destroyed, then rejuvenates with the next sunset and sends Yap to gather the PCs to her side once again—if she's ignored, she may turn her wrath against the citizens of Turtleback Ferry.

STATISTICS

Str —, **Dex** 20, **Con** —, **Int** 18, **Wis** 20, **Cha** 28

Base Atk +6; **Grp** —

Feats Ability Focus (blinding beauty), Combat Casting, Eschew Materials, Greater Spell Focus (evocation), Spell Focus (evocation)

Skills Concentration +15, Diplomacy +24, Escape Artist +20, Handle Animal +24, Heal +20, Hide +28, Listen +28, Move Silently +20, Search +12, Sense Motive +20, Spot +28

Languages Common, Sylvan

SQ rejuvenation, unearthly grace, wild empathy +27

Development: Myriana might be defeated, but her rage cannot be laid to rest until she recieves a fragment of Lamatar's body so she can *reincarnate* him. If the PCs defeat her, she cries out, "Return my beloved to me! Return my commander to my heart, or I shall find him with my vines and my dark trees will eat the land and churn your people to bone and misery. Return Lamatar to my embrace!" With that, her shade fades back into the waters, only to reform with the next setting of the sun.

PART FIVE: HARROWING THE HOOK

The great rains turn to driving snow as winter comes with a fury upon the Hook. Autumn is a forgotten dream as cutting wind lances through wool and leather, and treacherous ice crawls along the mountainside. Life is cruel and short on the Hook, more now than ever as winter sinks her teeth into its crags.

Reaching the base of Hook Mountain is no huge problem, but the last few miles include several frightening climbs. With a DC 20 Survival check, the PCs can follow hunting trails used by the Kreeg ogres and make the climb to the hold in three hours; but otherwise the party must make DC 15 Climb checks once per hour or be delayed an additional hour in their journey as they find the ice-laced trails and steep cliffs insurmountable—after making four successful Climb checks, they reach their goal. Random encounters with mountain-dwelling monsters (see page 71) can also serve to liven up this journey.

Snow falls for the duration of their trip, and the temperatures are cold. Consult the section on cold dangers in the DMG for more information on how the severe cold conditions affect the PCs.

Hook Mountain Clanhold

As the PCs finally crest the last craggy outcrop about a half-mile from Hook Mountain's 10,000-foot-high peak, they find a gaping cave belching forth foul black smoke. The cave entrance looks out over a wide ledge of windswept stone, while the chambers within are prowled by ogres aplenty, clutching their rusty hooks and constantly looking out for anyone foolish enough to encroach upon their den.

The clanhold itself is a large cave. The Kreegs have lived here for generations, and the walls and ceilings are thick with the soot of their fires. The caves are roomy, even for ogres. Passageways average 25 feet high, while the caverns themselves tend to have vaulted domelike ceilings up to 50 feet tall.

D1. Entrance (EL 10)

Constant flurries of wind-borne snow and frost lash at a gaping hole in the side of Hook Mountain here. Smoke pours forth from the cave entrance, only to be instantly dispersed by the wind.

Creatures: Two Kreeg fighters stand guard at the mouth of the clanhold, swathed in furs and leathers. Since news of Rannick's fall reached Barl's ears, things have been unpleasant in the hold, and these usually easily distracted ogres keep a sharp lookout. One was recently caught sleeping by Barl, and the stone giant tore off the lazy ogre's legs and left him rolling in the snow to bleed out before animating him as a zombie and turning him over to the three sisters for an eventual meal. These memories are enough to keep the Kreegs on alert for at least another week. Eager to prove to Barl that they can do a simple job like guarding the entrance, these two ogres don't think to raise an alarm until one is dead.

KREEG OGRES (2)   **CR 8**

Male ogre fighter 5

hp 90 each (see page 28)

D2. Bones of the Behemoth

At the mouth of darkness, jagged spurs of bone protrude from the stone on either side of the cave entrance, each towering twenty feet in height—apparently the ribs of some monstrous behemoth.

The bones of a blue dragon (identifiable as such with a successful DC 25 Knowledge [arcana] check) laid low by Kreeg ancestors still adorns the Clanholds' entryway, a testament to the once-mighty ogre mage overlords of Hook Mountain. The Kreegs have decorated the bones with crude scrimshaw carvings, incorporating the seven-pointed Sihedron Rune into the markings in many locations.

Hook Mountain
Clanhold

D8

D9

D7

D5

D4

D3

D2

To Mines

D6

D1

N

To Mines

One Square = 10 Feet

D3. The Rune-Bound King

An enormous statue stands here in frozen vigil—a forty-foot-tall giant with black skin covered by fissures and cracks, like the bed of a dried river. He wears majestic armor gilt and encrusted with gems, and grips a towering glaive in his armored fists. The giant's face is hidden by a ferocious full helm forged into the sneering grimace of a fanged devil. Around the giant's neck hangs a medallion—a seven-pointed star.

This gigantic "statue" is in fact a preserved body—the remains of the rune giant Gargadros, a one-time general in Karzoug's army. In the chaos that followed the fall of Thassilon, Gargadros seized Hook Mountain and the surrounding environs as his own, becoming the first of the line of Dread Kings. Grolki Kreeg claimed to be able to trace his heritage directly to this great warlord, a fact of which he was most proud. Draped around Gargadros's neck is a *Sihedron medallion*, its magic the sole thing that's preserved his flesh for the millennia the frozen corpse has stood here on display. When Barl arrived and revealed his own *Sihedron medallion*, Grolki fell to his knees in shock. The rune was once his family's mark, born on their faces or arms in testament to their eternal servitude to the archmage Karzoug. Grolki immediately swore allegiance to Barl and offered no resistance when Barl executed him moments later. From that point on, the Kreegs belonged to Breakbones.

Treasure: The *Sihedron medallion* around Gargadros's neck is sized for a Gargantuan creature and weighs 20 pounds, but still functions after all these years. *Sihedron medallions* are detailed in *Pathfinder #1* (apart from preserving corpses, they grant a +1 resistance bonus to saving throws and can be used once a day to cast *false life* as a free action at caster level 5th). The instant this medallion is removed from Gargadros, the ancient giant crumbles to dust and is gone; all that remains is his Gargantuan masterwork half-plate armor, which weighs 400 pounds and is worth 4,950 gp.

D4. The Burning Pit

A deep pit hewn from hard stone here descends into soot and darkness. The stale reek of decay wafts up from the depths below.

This is where the Kreegs formerly offered up sacrifices to Lamashtu, but now burn the rune-marked corpses of captives for their new liege-lord, Barl Breakbones. The PCs might think to clamber down the pit (DC 20 Climb check) to search for Lamatar's remains within, but all that waits for them 100 feet below is a swath of ash and shattered bone. Lamatar's body is not here.

D5. Chokepoint (EL 6)

Creatures: Three hulking ogres guard the entryway here under orders to raise an alarm if they detect intruders. If they do raise the alarm, they do their best to hold off intruders while the ogres in area **D6** gather weapons and come to their aid in

1d6 rounds. The denizens of areas **D7**–**D9** do not join battle here, preferring to face intruders in their lairs where they have stronger advantages.

Ogres (3)   CR 3

hp 29 each (MM 199)

D6. The Clanhold (EL 11)

Fire and thick black smoke reign here, spewing from black pits in the bedrock where forge fires glow. Anvils loom throughout this enormous cavern. The ring of steel on steel thunders here as giant hammers crash down again and again on glowing half-forged blades and axe-heads.

Once the Kreeg family den, this chamber was converted into a forge at Barl's order. Many more ogres toil deep in the bowels of Hook Mountain, in cave mines hundreds of feet below. These ogres are too distant and exhausted to be of any aid to those in the caves above when the PCs arrive, but could be used as reinforcements if the PCs retreat from the Hold and come back later.

Creatures: A work crew of eight ogres slaves away here, toiling endlessly at these forges to craft giant blades and other weapons from the obstinate iron they've carved from the mountain's innards. They are all exhausted. Their two Kreeg ogre taskmasters snarl, belch, guffaw, and roar incessantly. The Kreegs order the exhausted ogres to attack any intruders, laughing as the weary ogres stumble to their deaths. The Kreegs then snatch up red-hot half-forged blades and go to work as well (inflicting an additional 1d6 fire damage with each hit).

Kreeg Ogres (2)

Male ogre fighter 5
hp 90 (see page 28)

Exhausted Ogres (8)   CR 3

Male ogre barbarian 4
hp 29 each (MM 199)

D7. Circle of the Sisters (EL 9)

This foul-smelling cave is cluttered with an appalling amount of body parts, dead animals, spoiled food, and filth, but none so hideous as what bubbles and cooks in a huge cauldron over a sputtering fire in a nook to the north.

Creatures: This cavern is the foul redoubt of the Sisters of the Hook—a covey of annis hags who have long served as allies of and consorts to the Kreeg clan. Now that Grolki is dead, the hags aren't sure what to make of Barl, who appreciates their skills

but is repulsed by their appearances. For now, they work with the stone giant, but suspect he doesn't have their best interests in his heart. The sisters know all too well that they are short on allies.

Rumor holds that these three annis hags were once related to princess Myriana before envy and evil jealousy polluted them and they engaged in all manner of monstrous acts and vile rites in hopes of improving their beauty to outshine their sister. Briselda is a hulking humpbacked hag with oversized talons sprouting from her stumpy arms. Grelthaga is tall and thin, like a skeleton wrapped in ugly purple flesh and a sagging white robe. Larastine's face is a mass of pustules, warts the size of gold pieces, and craters that weep ooze. She is squat and fat with bulbous breasts that hang almost to her knees. The sisters see each other for the horrors they are, but in their madness, they see their own reflections as pure loveliness.

The hags are attended by their newest pet—the undead body of Lamatar Bayden. Barl was quite pleased after he finished torturing the one-time commander of Fort Rannick with necromantic techniques he learned from his master Mokmurian and gave him over to the three hags as a servant in reward for

LAMATAR BAYDEN

their aid in bringing the rains to the region. Lamatar's body is caked with ice; his left hand looks almost to be a claw made of icicles and his brow is decorated with a crown of the same.

BRISELDA, GRELTHAGA, AND LARASTINE   CR 6

Annis hags

hp 45 each (MM 143)

TACTICS

Before Combat All three hags are protected by *mind blank*.

During Combat The hags are nearly ready to abandon the Kreegs, but if intruders confront them here, they put up a fight for a few rounds, favoring their more powerful covey spell-like abilities like *bestow curse* and *forcecage* at the start of the fight before finishing things off with their melee attacks.

Morale If any of the hags are dropped below 15 hit points, all three attempt to flee the clanhold. If prevented from doing so, they beg for their lives and might even be convinced to aid the PCs in a fight with Barl.

LAMATAR BAYDEN   CR 3

Wight

hp 26 (MM 255)

TACTICS

During Combat Lamatar retains no trace of his living personality, and follows the orders of his three mistresses without question.

Morale Lamatar fights to the death.

D8. Abandoned Shrine

A shrine bearing the feral visage of a brutally beautiful monstrous maiden with the head of a three-eyed jackal and the belly of a pregnant young woman leans against the far wall.

This was once the Kreegs' well-tended shrine to Lamashtu, but now that Barl has arrived and their old leader Grolki is dead, no Kreeg has visited this shrine recently.

D9. As the Dread Kings of Old (EL 12)

This gigantic chamber extends into darkness to the east, sloping upward between two wide ledges on which loom statues of angular faces, strong brows, and fixed jawlines. Above, the ceiling opens up to the slate-gray sky above. The ramp leads up in tiers, finally coming to an end before an immense stone throne.

Creatures: Once the throne room for Grolki Kreeg, this open-air cleft in the lee of Hook Mountain's summit has become Barl Breakbones's den. He has taken to the role of overlord with excess, and has delayed the gathering of weaponry for Mokmurian simply to extend his time here as king. Originally, Barl was attended by two bodyguards, but when one of them commented that perhaps Barl needed to step up his schedule and get this army of disgusting ogres back to Mokmurian, Barl had that one executed. The remaining stone giant guard has wisely held his counsel to himself.

Barl sighs wearily before waving an arm at his remaining bodyguard, saying (in Giant), "Deal with these mites. They've caused enough problems for me."

BARL BREAKBONES   CR 11

Male stone giant necromancer 7

NE Large giant (earth)

Init +1; **Senses** darkvision 60 ft., low-light vision; Listen +21, Spot +21

DEFENSE

AC 25, touch 10, flat-footed 24

    (+4 armor, +1 Dex, +11 natural, –1 size)

hp 164 (177 with *false life*; 14d8+7d4+84)

Fort +16, **Ref** +8, **Will** +12

Defensive Abilities rock catching; **Resist** cold 10

OFFENSE

Spd 40 ft.

Melee mwk earth breaker +23/+18/+13 (3d6+13/19–20/×3)

Ranged rock +13 (2d8+13)

Space 10 ft.; **Reach** 10 ft.

Special Attacks rock throwing

Spells Known (CL 7th; 8th with necromancy spells, +13 ranged touch)

    4th—*animate dead, fear* (DC 19)

    3rd—*fly, ray of exhaustion, vampiric touch* (2)

    2nd—*blindness/deafness* (DC 17), *command undead, false life, ghoul touch* (DC 17), *spectral hand*

    1st—*chill touch* (DC 16), *mage armor, magic missile* (3), *ray of enfeeblement*

    0—*touch of fatigue* (5, DC 15)

    Prohibited Schools abjuration, enchantment

TACTICS

Before Combat Barl starts every day by casting *false life* and *mage armor* on himself; if the PCs arrive late at night, these spell effects have expired and you should reduce his AC by four points and his hit points by 13. If Barl hears the sounds of combat nearby, he stations his stone giant bodyguard near the entrance. Once that guard notices PCs approaching, he calls out to Barl, who casts *fly* and *spectral hand* if he has the chance.

During Combat Barl would rather let his bodyguard fight his fights while he remains seated on his throne, casting spells from there. If the PCs manage to reach him in melee, he sighs heavily, lifts his earth breaker, and responds in kind. If one of the PCs is killed, Barl gets a gleam in his eye and casts *animate dead* on the body the first chance he gets, more to see the anguish of the new zombie's one-time allies than out of any real sense of tactics.

Morale Barl is no stranger to death, but does not want to go there himself. If reduced to less than 15 hit points, the giant drops his weapon and begs for his life. He's willing to reveal much of what Mokmurian has planned for the region if the PCs are willing to grant him mercy (see Concluding the Adventure, below).

STATISTICS

Str 29, **Dex** 12, **Con** 18, **Int** 17, **Wis** 14, **Cha** 14

Base Atk +13; **Grp** +26

Feats Alertness (as long as Vizarka is in arm's reach), Combat Casting, Greater Spell Focus (necromancy), Improved Bull Rush, Improved Critical (earth breaker), Eschew Materials, Power Attack, Scribe

Scroll, Spell Focus (necromancy), Spell Mastery (*fly, mage armor, magic missile*), Weapon Focus (earth breaker)

Skills Climb +29, Concentration +14, Hide +14 (+22 in rocky terrain), Knowledge (arcana) +10, Knowledge (religion) +10, Listen +21, Spellcraft +12, Spot +21

Languages Common, Draconic, Giant, Thassilonian

SQ summon familiar (lizard named Vizarka)

Combat Gear *wand of enervation* (12 charges); **Other Gear** masterwork earth breaker, *ring of minor cold resistance, Sihedron medallion*, 650 gp in black onyx gems, spellbook (contains only those spells prepared)

STONE GIANT   CR 8

hp 45 (MM 143)

CONCLUDING THE ADVENTURE

With the defeat of Barl Breakbones, the PCs not only free the Kreegs from being enslaved and pressed into war but prevent further assaults on the region—now leaderless, the Kreegs themselves are weak and vulnerable. Those who survive the PCs' visit scatter into the wilds of Hook Mountain. The lucky ones find new homes with other ogre tribes, but most fall prey to these same tribes as there is no love lost between the ogres of the Hook.

If the PCs defeat the undead Lamatar and return with his body (or even just a portion of it) to Myriana, the nymph is overjoyed and casts *reincarnate* upon him. As she does, her undead spirit fades and the curse on Whitewillow withers. Lamatar is at first shamed by his failure to protect both Fort Rannick and his lover, but decides not to waste the new life she gave him. He becomes the new guardian of Whitewillow and does not return to civilization.

If the PCs capture Barl Breakbones alive, it shouldn't take much to convince the craven giant to talk. Barl's eagerness to tell the PCs about his lord Mokmurian, and how he is gathering an army of giants to march on Varisia, could be mistaken for pride in his master's plot, when in fact Barl is simply desperate to please the PCs so that they'll let him live. Barl himself is from a smaller tribe deep in the Iron Peaks, and although he's never been inside Jorgenfist, the fabled fortress of the stone giants and the lair of his master Mokmurian, he can certainly provide the PCs with directions to it.

For now, the PCs have earned a rest. Feel free to give them days, weeks, or even months. Maintaining Fort Rannick can certainly keep them diverted for some time if they wish to stay on as the keep's commanders, or they may wish to return home to Sandpoint to winter there. Shalelu does the latter, and if the PCs decide to stay at Fort Rannick, they'll eventually receive a disturbing message from their elven ranger ally—stone giants have been sighted west of Ember Lake, and fears are that a platoon of them might be headed for Sandpoint. Can the PCs return to their home in time to aid in its defense against the vanguard of an army of giants?

KEEPING THE KEEP

RUNNING A FORTRESS IN VARISIA AND BEYOND

Daunting edifices of rulership and martial might, every castle carries with it a story. From seats of royalty to ruins of legend, lairs of monsters to tenuous bastions of civilization, countless adventures might stem from these intimidating fortresses or take place within their cold, unyielding walls. Yet few heroes might expect that, aside from laying siege to or delving through a castle, running such a fortress can be an adventure all its own. Yet, before one takes up the mantle of lordship, one should know what has come before and what dangers such a title might entail.

Few things evoke a more iconic medieval feeling than a castle. While the exact definition of a castle remains somewhat debated, in general terms a true castle distinguishes itself from similar structures by a mixture of purposes. A castle serves as both an administrative building and a residence, housing the lord of the land and his support staff. When attacked, nearby farmers and villagers can retreat to the castle for protection, as provided for in the basic tenets of feudalism. A castle can also act as an offensive weapon, laying claim to hostile territory in an effort to expand control or suppress dissension. In this case, a king or emperor can extend his territories by building a castle and emplacing a loyal lord who will make sure the royal will is carried out.

A BRIEF HISTORY OF CASTLES

Castles as defensive structures have a lengthy history in the real world. Long before the development of crenellations and concentric defenses, predating even the motte-and-bailey design, the earliest defensive structures consisted of earthworks reinforced with wooden walls. These precursors served exclusively as defensive forts and lacked the greater strategic value of castles. Romans perfected the practices of both building and defeating forts, and over time some of these Roman forts grew into true castles.

Beginning in the 9th century, the Carolingian Empire constructed castles to defend its frontiers and as palatial homes for its nobles and royalty. As the Carolingian Empire collapsed and chaos spread again in Western Europe, new castles—utilizing the motte-and-bailey technique—rose across the lands of modern-day France. The Normans who invaded England in 1066 brought this fundamental castle design with them, spreading the motte-and-bailey technique around England and eventually into Ireland.

In the 10th and 11th centuries, Western Europeans encountered for the first time the impressive fortifications in use within both the Byzantine Empire (including the massive Walls of Constantinople, which repelled all attacks for a thousand years) and the Islamic empires occupying the Holy Land. This influx of advanced defensive engineering led to the implementation of multiple concentric defenses, the rounding of walls (angled corners are far more susceptible to sapping), and the proliferation of castles built on flat ground rather than on hills or mounds.

With the coming of gunpowder, the dominance of castles began quickly to wane. Before they completely lost their value as defensive structures, though, castles evolved yet again to resist these new threats. Walls thickened and bulged and the beautiful aesthetics of high, majestic towers gave way to more practical considerations. Eventually, though, the destructive development of cannons outpaced the innovations of castles, leading to the demise of castles as multiuse structures around the 16th century. Beginning as early as the 14th century, castles and structures like them lost their military roles and became little more than beautiful manor houses.

CASTLE FEATURES

As individual as the lords who commission them, castles nonetheless share some similarities, and many contain the following features.

PEOPLE IN A CASTLE

Castles require and house many different kinds of people. Some of the most important people in a castle include the following.

Bailiff: Oversees peasants and repairs to buildings.

Castellan: Custodian of the castle (not always the lord).

Chamberlain: The castellan's personal accountant and keeper of the great chamber (the lord's bedroom).

Chaplain: Tends the chapel and oversees the spiritual well-being of all castle residents.

Clerk: Bookkeeper.

Constable: Caretaker of the castle when the castellan is away. Considered a great honor for royal castles.

Domestic Servants: Bottlers, the butler (cellar supervisor), cooks, cottars (laborers), ewerers (hot-water bearers), gong farmers (latrine cleaners), haywards (hedge-tenders), and porters (door-wardens).

Falconer: Cares for and trains the lord's hunting hawks.

Herald: An expert on heraldry and an assistant to the castle's knights.

Knight: A life-long professional soldier whose training began as a small child.

Lord: The owner and primary resident of the castle. Can be nobility or royalty.

Reeve: The senior supervisor of the lord's property. Manages all work on the castle.

Seneschal: The senior domestic supervisor. Manages the household (including servants) and runs events in the great hall. Sometimes called the steward.

Squire: An adolescent knight-in-training assigned to aid and carry weapons for an established knight.

Tradesmen: Atilliators (crossbow-makers), blacksmiths, carpenters, cordwainers (shoe-makers), ditchers (ditch-diggers), dyers, the keeper of the wardrobe (tailor and laundress supervisor), the marshal (horse-keeper), the master mason, weavers, and woodworkers.

Watchman: A soldier concerned with security and a member of the castle's garrison.

Barbican: An extension of the enceinte (see below) surrounding the castle's main entrance, the barbican adds another layer of defense against attackers attempting a frontal assault.

Bastion: This small tower along a curtain wall gives the castle's soldiers a greater field of view, allowing them to defend the walls more effectively.

Enceinte: Also known as curtain walls, the enceintes form the outer defenses of castles. Many castles provide additional protection to their walls with towers. The largest and best-defended castles possess multiple concentric enceintes.

Hoardings: Walls provide excellent passive defenses, but in times of siege they can be easily overcome. Temporary wooden walkways known as hoardings, built on the inside of castle walls, allow defenders to fire arrows or drop boiling oil onto invaders below. When permanently built—usually of stone—hoardings are called machicolations.

Keep: The last line of defense, the keep is the best-defended part of the castle. It usually houses the lord of the castle, as well as many of his guards, his family, and his closest and most trusted servants.

Motte-and-Bailey: A motte is a hill, often manmade, upon which stands a defensive structure, such as a keep. Surrounding the motte is a bailey, an enclosed courtyard housing support structures (such as stables, servants' housing, forges, and the like), protected by a wall. The surrounding wall can be made of wood or stone, depending on the technological advancement and wealth of the builder.

Other Defenses: Battlements and crenellations provide cover for defenders but allow them room to fire arrows and drop oil. Murder holes and embrasures are tall but narrow slits in walls that give archers a wide field of view and maximum cover. A moat is a deep trench, often filled with water, which surrounds all or most of the castle.

THE BURDEN OF RULE

Any organization or community—whether it be a fortress, village, or business—requires a leader to take charge and assure its smooth day-to-day workings. If the PCs take control of Fort Rannick and decide to maintain it as a working community, they might find the complexities of running the fortress deeply rewarding or surprisingly deadly. GMs should feel free to present their newly landed PCs with any of the encounters described in the following section or create their own specific problems or events to add excitement to the business of running a keep. Alternately, if a GM feels that the abilities and skills of the characters themselves should have a direct influence over whether or not their fortress flourishes, presented here is a simple system to quantify the PCs' ability to rule. While Fort Rannick is used as a default throughout this discussion, feel free to adapt this simple system to any community the PCs attempt to manage.

WEEKLY FORTRESS EVENTS

d20	Event		
1	Attack	11	Have At You!
2	Fire	12–18	No Event
3	Collapsing Tower	19	Secret Chamber
4	Fouled Waters	20	Varisian Wanderers
5–7	No Event	21	Merchant Deal
8	Stalking Monster	22–24	No Event
9	Snake Oil Salesman	25	Local Gift
10	Hero Problems	26+	Welcome Travelers

While the PCs are in residence at Fort Rannick, the party should select one character to be the lord, the manager of the keep. Once per week, the lord makes a Charisma check and applies the result to the chart in the Weekly Fortress Events sidebar to see what encounter or event arises in the coming week. High rolls result in benefits and good fortunes, while low rolls reveal problems and calamities. A character with the Leadership feat (see page 106 of the DMG) gains a +2 bonus on this roll. GMs should feel free to apply ad hoc modifiers to a character's weekly event roll as circumstances within the campaign dictate or simply to flavor an uneventful or repetitive series of results.

If the PCs choose to depart from their fortress but plan to return and retake control, they should consider leaving an NPC in charge. A cohort gained through the Leadership feat would

REBUILDING THE KEEP

Even once the PCs have managed to secure themselves a castle, there's still plenty of work to be done. Below are several ideas for handling the repair and maintenance necessary for a working fortress.

When making repairs, tasks fall into two categories: those requiring pure labor, and those that necessitate a certain amount of expertise. For gruntwork such as cleaning or clearing fallen debris, tasks are generally measured in man-hours—as soon as one or more people have put in a certain amount of time, the task is completed. For complex tasks like repairing a hole in a curtain wall or shoring up sagging supports in the great hall, each task is instead assigned a Craft DC and a gp value. A character or artisan working on a given task is finished when the value of his crafting—as detailed in the description of the Craft skill in the PHB—equals the value of the repair. The hole in the curtain wall, for instance, might require a character to make repeated DC 15 Craft (stoneworking) checks until the value of the repairs reaches 200 gp, while repairing a few rotted timbers might only require 75 gp worth of DC 15 Craft (carpentry) checks. Characters with Knowledge (architecture and engineering) can help plan repairs by making a check equal to the DC of the related Craft check, reducing the overall gp price of repairs by 10%.

For characters uninterested in doing the work themselves, hiring help is always an option. Unskilled laborers work for 1 sp per 8 hours of labor, while carpenters or stonemasons cost 3 sp per day and can be assumed to do 27 sp worth of work in that time. In the case of Fort Rannick, the nearby town of Turtleback Ferry should have all the workers PCs might need to renovate their new fortress. Bear in mind that the price of materials for any project, as listed in the PH, is the owner's responsibility.

be the optimal choice, as such a character is typically devoted to the PCs and does not demand payment. If the PCs don't have a cohort they wish to leave behind, they might hire a steward or overseer to maintain the fortress in their absence. A typical steward is capable of sustaining the status quo at a keep, but is not exceptional and will not improve the characters' holdings. It should be assumed that the steward always rolls a 15 (No Event) on the Weekly Fortress Events chart. On average, a steward charges 50 gp per month for his work, payable upon the PCs' return. Should he not hear from the characters for more than six months, he likely abandons the keep—along with all the fortress's workers—unless he is particularly devoted to the PCs or they have some prior arrangement. If a GM wishes to have some windfall or calamity befall the keep during the steward's management, he should feel free to do so, but such development should be worked into a greater story lest the PCs feel that they are being treated unfairly.

If the PCs leave their keep without relinquishing control to another leader or a steward abandons it, the fortress quickly deteriorates and is likely overrun by some hostile element—such as brigands, Shoanti barbarians, ogres, or other menaces—presenting a dangerous problem for PCs to deal with upon their return.

Attack

When this event begins, the PC lord must make a DC 20 Gather Information check. If he succeeds, he learns that a hostile band of brigands or savage humanoids is mustering its forces to make an attack on Fort Rannick. The attack force will arrive in 2d6 days, and the PCs have that time to make themselves and the fort ready for battle.

When the enemy arrives, the GM should run the siege as a series of events, giving the PCs a combination of encounters meant to test both their skills and their combat prowess—along with those of any allies or hired aid. The GM should gauge the party's effectiveness through these encounters to determine how well the enemy attack is confronted. Aside from battling outright on the fortress walls, rallying demoralized soldiers, extinguishing fires set by flaming arrows, or detecting a saboteur might be but a few challenges put before the defenders.

Depending on how the PCs perform, the fortress might require several weeks of repairs during which other enemies might attack the weakened fort. Should the PCs deal with the attack exceedingly well or poorly, enemies might be reluctant to attack the castle or, alternatively, overwhelm the keep and force the party to flee.

Fire

A lantern kicked over in the castle stable catches the surrounding straw on fire, and before long the entire structure is in flames. Making things worse, one of the young grooms gets stuck beneath a fallen beam as he raced to rescue the horses.

From the moment the PCs reach the stable, they have 4 rounds to rescue the unconscious groom before he dies of smoke inhalation. Locating him requires a DC 15 Search check, and lifting the heavy beam off of him requires a DC 17 Strength check. Each round, a character inside the burning building must make a DC 15 Reflex save or take 1d4 points of fire damage.

Characters can put out the fire by organizing a bucket brigade with a DC 20 Diplomacy or Intimidate check, or use magic such as *quench* or summoned water elementals (the fire is too large for *gust of wind* or *pyrotechnics* to be effective). If the party is unable to get the fire put out in short order, it completely destroys the stables and several other outbuildings before burning out. If this occurs or the groom dies, the staff's confidence in their lord is severely shaken. Rerolling this event results in a similarly destructive accident.

Collapsing Tower

One of the fort's towers unexpectedly collapses! Several residents are killed and others are injured. Craftsmen at work in the fortress are demoralized and, unless the PCs improve morale, they work at half of their normal speed. A DC 15 Diplomacy or Perform check made in the morning can bolster the moods of the workers for one day, allowing them to produce a full day's worth of work. Four successful checks in a row permanently restore their spirits. Failing a Perform check increases the DC for all following checks by 2, and failing five times (in total) before making four successful checks in a row completely demoralizes the workers, who quit the next day, requiring the lord to spend at least a week searching out new craftsmen.

Fouled Waters

A period of heavy rain causes corruption and disease from the fort's cesspool to seep into the nearby water source, making residents sick with filth fever. As the water is being continually polluted, the local priests are helpless to purify it; they recommend digging a new well at the farthest possible point within the keep's walls, a task with a Craft (stoneworking or carpentry) DC of 15 and a cost of 75 gp. Repeat rolls with this result turn up similar costly chores related to the fortress, such as the digging of a new latrine, reroofing structures, or shoring up sagging walls.

Stalking Monster

A troll hunter named **Karraktuksch** (CE male troll ranger 6; MM 247) has taken up residence in a nearby copse of Varisian white firs. A brigand with a fierce hunger, the troll preys on those coming to and from the fortress. If he is not dealt with swiftly, the roads leading to the fort gain a dangerous reputation and workers and travellers shun them, potentially even after the monster is dispatched.

Rerolling this event results in other monstrous infestations, such as aggressive ankhegs, hunting manticores, marauding owlbears, or even a young dragon.

Snake Oil Salesman

Dwarven trader **Silas Tor** (NE male dwarf adept 3/expert 4; Bluff +10, Diplomacy +10) cuts a fine figure as he rides through the gates astride his miniature donkey, excited children running in the wake of his cart heaped with goods. Within minutes of his arrival, he manages to attract a sizable crowd in the castle yard where he stands atop his cart, eloquently expounding on the wonders of his assorted relics and knick-knacks, all guaranteed to perform miracles from curing illnesses to helping one find her true love without paying the exorbitant prices of a wizard or cleric. As his patter washes over the crowd, those assembled begin mustering their hard-earned wages and handing them over with hopeful, trusting expressions.

Silas's baubles are, of course, useless junk enhanced with minor illusion magic; this fast-talking con artist moves from town to town hawking his wares. In order for the PCs to chase off or arrest the scoundrel, they must first recognize his fraud with a DC 14 Knowledge (arcana) check, a DC 14 Spellcraft check, or a Sense Motive attempt opposed by the dwarf's Bluff skill. They can then take action against Silas, but need to make a Diplomacy or Intimidate check (opposed by Silas's Bluff if his wares aren't proved fraudulent, DC 15 if they are) to keep the crowd from objecting and potentially swarming the cart. Silas, for his part, attempts to use his remaining spells to flee if revealed as a fraud.

If this event is rerolled, a similarly troublesome visitor turns up at the fort, such as a fiery evangelist of Iomedae, a Magnimarian tax collector, or a hellknight looking to "clean up" Fort Rannick.

Hero Problems

Everyone is ecstatic when famed giant-killer **Terek "Earthbreaker" Charhok** (N male human fighter 8) elects to grace the keep with his presence while waiting out some inclement weather. Simply having him at their table makes folk feel like part of a fairy tale, and his own stories are easily worth the cost of the ale he drinks. As the weeks grind on, however, the excitement begins to wear thin, and people rankle at his imperious manner, poor table manners, and drain on the castle's stores. Now, with not one but two different scullery maids pregnant by the "hero," it falls to the lord of the castle to oust the ingrate before he does any further damage.

Rerolling this result might mean Charhok returns, either to shack up with his old friends again or seeking vengeance, depending on how he was dismissed. Alternately, after hearing how well Earthbreaker was treated, the hero's old and equally uncouth adventuring companions might show up at the PCs' front door.

Have At You!

In celebration of an important holiday, it's customary for prominent land owners to host a feast and tournament for their tenants, inviting everyone for miles around to come enjoy their hospitality and compete in feats of strength and skill. Each year, all comers are allowed to compete with each other in a friendly joust, archery contest, or wizard's duel, according to the whim of the keep's rulers. Tradition then dictates that the lord or a champion of his choosing must challenge the victor. If the lord wins, the challenger is offered a reward of 100 gp from the lord's personal funds, but if the challenger wins, he's paid 500 gp and potentially offered a position on the lord's staff. The GM and PCs should feel free to organize and play through the events of the festival as they please, but the climax is likely a competition with the tournament's most skilled challenger, a character roughly equivalent to the lord in level and class.

Secret Chamber

A jarring tremor disrupts the daily routine at Fort Rannick. While the quake lasts only a moment, passing with little damage and no casualties, a previously unknown chamber is revealed in the fort's basement. What lies within—whether it be a hidden vault, a deadly secret, or a passage to depths and dangers in the earth below—is left for the GM to decide.

Varisian Wanderers

The brightly painted wagons of a Varisian caravan roll up to the fort. The clan's patron, **Jarrim Kovini** (N male human ranger 5), seeks a place for his people to rest and resupply and treats with the PCs for their hospitality. Should the PCs allow the wanderers to stay, the caravan sets up camp by the nearby waterfall, and the following nights are filled with dancing, song, and strange Varisian customs (see page 67). Whether this unexpected carnival atmosphere is a boon or a curse, though, depends on the events of the coming days. While the entertainment alone might be welcome, the Varisians might actually be Sczarni thieves, or a guard at the fortress might elope with Jarrim's daughter (inciting the protective caravan leader's fury). How the PCs respond to any of these possibilities determine whether the nomads leave as new friends or curse-shouting foes.

Merchant Deal

Members of a trading concern with interests in the surrounding mountains approach the PCs hoping to strike a deal. The merchants would like to use Fort Rannick as a stop to resupply their caravans and store goods, and are willing to offer up to 100 gp a month for the PCs' cooperation. While the deal seems to be easy money, who these merchants represent could significantly change the fortress's prospects. While simple miners or representatives of Janderhoff could make fine business partners, more unscrupulous businessmen, like envoys of the Aspis Consortium, could be involved in far more dangerous dealings.

CASTLES OF VARISIA

As Chelaxian settlers are relatively new residents of the region, and both the Shoanti and native Varisians embrace a more nomadic lifestyle, there are few true keeps and castles in modern Varisia. Several of the more notable castles are detailed below.

The Arvensoar: A key element in Magnimar's defenses, the Arvensoar houses much of the city's militia and enough supplies to keep the populace from starving during anything short of a major siege.

Castle Korvosa: Built on top of a massive, flat-topped pyramid, Castle Korvosa is the decadent yet impregnable seat of the Korvosan royalty.

Citadel Vraid: From the Mindspin Mountains south of Korvosa, the black, horn-crowned bastion of the hellknight Order of the Nail casts its shadow of mercilessness and absolute law.

Fort Rannick: A sturdy frontier fortress near the intimidating slopes of Hook Mountain. Based here, The Order of the Black Arrow defends the surrounding region from the predations of ogres and worse. See "The Hook Mountain Massacre" for more details.

Fort Veldraine: This spartan, heavily-fortified complex houses an enormous winch capable of raising a great chain across the mouth of Conquerer's Bay, sealing Korvosa off from the rest of the Arcadian Ocean.

Twilight Academy: Although this college of the arcane in Galduria has rarely seen the need to close its gates, its architects incorporated numerous magical and mundane defenses into its design, seemingly better constructed to keep residents in than to repel invaders.

Viperwall: Little is known about this sinister fortress at the edge of Ember Lake, but most speculators agree that no human hands crafted its strange, serpent-carved ramparts.

Windsong Abbey: Although dedicated to fostering understanding between the followers of Varisia's major deities, the monks of Windsong Abbey are not blind to rising tensions in the region, and keep the walls of their towering monastery in good repair.

Local Gift

Good fortune shines upon one of the fortress's residents or the PCs themselves. A small vein of precious metal is found nearby, a bribe from Magnimar or Korvosa shows up, a known brigand turns himself in, or a local holiday brings gift-bearing travelers to the keep. Regardless of the form it takes, the PCs gain a gift worth approximately 500 gp.

Welcome Travelers

Friendly settlers, sociable nobles, skilled craftsmen, wandering priestesses, explorers, Pathfinders, or other welcome travelers learn of the fortress's respected reputation and pay a visit, bringing news, samples of their crafts, gifts, or rumors of possible adventures. Whatever the specifics of these passersby, their presence should be a boon to the PCs.

VARISIA

CRADLE OF LEGENDS

Dotted with the monolithic relics of an empire long since crumbled, Varisia is a rough but majestic land, its misty forests and rolling plains bordered by sharp peaks and bountiful seas. Its people, recently released from colonialism, are hardy frontiersmen and new-money nobles, all eager to carve names for themselves from Varisia's stern landscape. Yet beyond their village borders, beasts and giants unused to civilization's encroachment stalk the hills and woods, making short work of the unwary and legends of the bold.

What follows is a gazetteer of the region known as Varisia. While much of this rugged land remains unexplored, what little is known tempts the daring and holds the potential for untold adventure. For fortune-hunters, Varisia is a land of limitless opportunity, its ancient monuments reminding them just how far the driven can rise.

Ashwood: While many forests in Varisia bear dark reputations, Ashwood's is legendary. Everyone within a hundred miles claims to have a relative or friend-of-a-friend who personally encountered a ghost, werewolf, or other spook within the wood's brooding borders. Yet while locals might boast excitedly and exchange tales by day, at night they bar their doors and pile firewood high. The Church of Erastil takes these stories particularly seriously, and worshipers of Ol' Deadeye are frequently seen patrolling the dells and towns along the forest's ragged edge, making sure the dark creatures within its borders stay there.

Bloodsworn Vale: The site of a bloody engagement between invading Chelish forces and desperate Shoanti barbarians, Bloodsworn Vale was a primary trade route between Cheliax and its Varisian colonies. It fell into disuse after the empire's collapse. As a few Varisian port cities grow increasingly wealthy from southern trade, many land-locked towns have begun clamoring for the pass to be reopened. For more information, see *GameMastery Module W1: Conquest of Bloodsworn Vale*.

Brinewall: Originally settled by Chelaxians out of Korvosa, and once the northernmost Chelish holding in Varisia, this fortress was perfectly situated to defend against and facilitate trade with the harsh warriors from the Lands of the Linnorm Kings. Despite the constant threat of Nolander barbarians, the dragon-helmed militia manning the fort's eponymous curtain wall proved more than capable of rebuffing attacks. Twenty years ago, however, all communication with the fortress stopped. Investigations revealed an empty citadel, devoid of all evidence of attack or disaster. Although most blame the Nolanders, the complete absence of bodies and pristine shape of the empty ships bobbing in the harbor speak toward a more sinister calamity.

Calphiak Mountains: The Calphiak Mountains are the youngest range in Varisia, dating back a mere 10,000 years to the cataclysmic end of the Thassilonian Empire. Today, the mountains are renowned for their high concentration of Thassilonian artifacts, most famously the Valley of Stars, a heavily etched crater many explorers believe to be a massive celestial observatory.

Celwynvian: Deep in the Mierani forest, the ancient elven capital of Celwynvian stands empty, its verdant palaces and delicate towers poised breathlessly in the half-light beneath the canopy. Avoided superstitiously by other races during the elves' long absence, the City of Emerald Rains has been quarantined since their return. Refusing all requests by outsiders to enter their ancestral home, the elves claim to have cut off the city to provide their kind with a refuge from the outside world. Those who deal with the denizens of the Mierani forest, however, whisper that the elves themselves actually reside outside the city, fighting a hidden war to retake their capital from a sinister and unnamed force.

TRIBES OF THE SHOANTI

Seven tribes of Shoanti roam the harshest environments in Varisia.

Lyrune-Quah: The Clan of the Moon wanders the open lands east of the Wyvern Mountains. Resolute and cold, its members have long fought with the giants of the Kodar Mountains.

Shadde-Quah: The Clan of the Axe lives a secluded life in the coastal valleys of the Calphiak Mountains, raiding ships that come near its shores and doing much to guard Varisia's coast from nautical incursions from the Lands of the Linnorm Kings.

Shriikirri-Quah: The Clan of the Hawk ranges far in its travels, from the Gnashers to the Churlwood. Its members hold great respect for animals and claim to learn much from their ways.

Shundar-Quah: The diplomats of the Shoanti, the Clan of the Spire wanders across the northern Storval Plateau, ever seeking to unite the tribes into a single people. The tribesmen claim to be the heart of the Shoanti and to know the secrets of their past.

Sklar-Quah: The people of the Cinderlands, the warlike Clan of the Sun has suffered much at the hands of orcs and Chelish invaders. Endlessly bent on revenge, they brook no trespassers.

Skoan-Quah: The small and mysterious Clan of the Skull travels widely through the Cinderlands and the northern plateau, keeping record of the tribes that have passed and honoring the dead in all things.

Tamiir-Quah: The reclusive Clan of the Wind haunts the Stony Mountains. Distrustful and quick to take offense, its warriors claim all the lands within sight of their mountains as their home.

Chorak's Tomb: The giants of the Storval Plateau were not always the barbarians they are today, and perhaps the best proof of this lies on the tiny island in Lake Skotha known to the giants as Chorak's Tomb. Here, it is rumored, the descendants of the giant warlord's honor guard still cling to the remnants of civilization, protecting the last traces of their race's glory. All of this remains speculation, however, as any sentient creatures attempting to approach the island are bombarded with rocks or shot down with rune-carved ballista bolts. Not even other giants know what secrets lie at the island's center, and for now, beyond a few glints of metallic structures in the distance, the mystery of Chorak's Tomb goes unanswered.

Churlwood: A tangled forest choked by tenacious vines, Churlwood is almost impossible for non-natives to navigate, making it the perfect refuge for the bandit gangs and goblin tribes that raid from its borders. With its plentiful game and renowned ability to confuse even the most canny trackers, the wood is a popular destination for wanted men, its borders a haven for rogues and escaped slaves alike—hence the expression, "Safe as a thief in Churlwood." Of course, what the stories of outlaw folk heroes and egalitarian bandits fail to mention is just how many men who enter the forest are never seen again.

Cinderlands: The Cinderlands take up the majority of the southern Storval Plateau, its dry, ashen soil approaching desert status in many places. Many of the plants here require fire to split open their seedpods, and in the summer, wildfires race across the

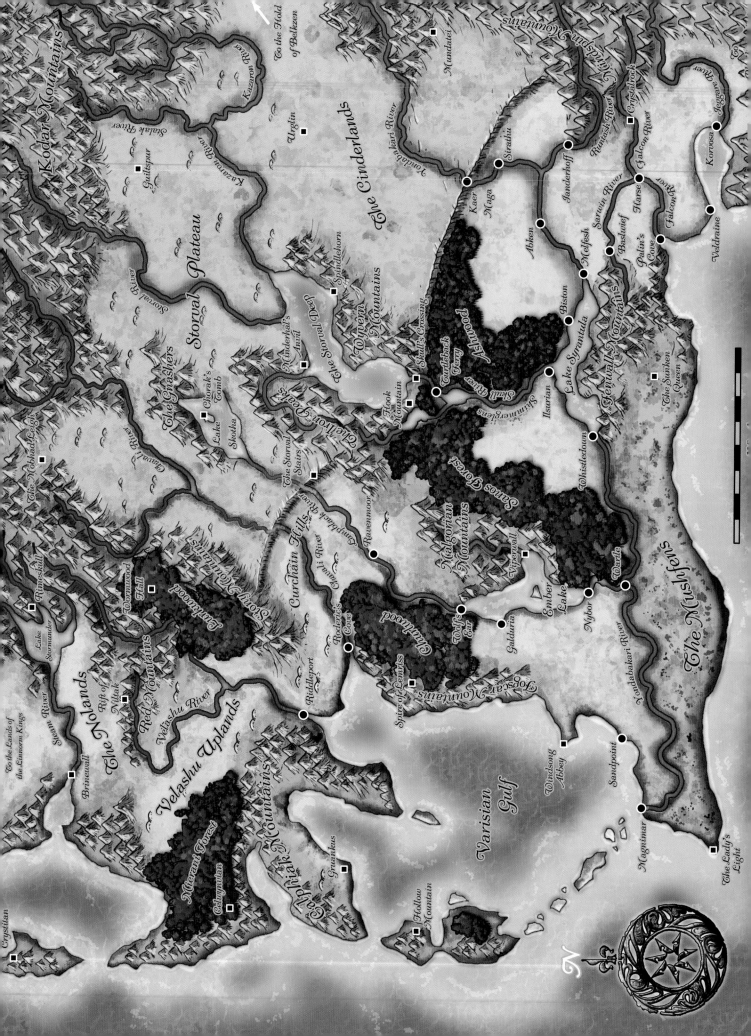

badlands in vast sheets of flame ignited by the ferocious seasonal thunderstorms. In these harsh environs, only the Shoanti make any real settlements, and these generally consist of yurts and other easily transportable structures. Fire plays a central role in the lives of these upland tribes as well, and many promote harsh right-of-passage rituals in which young warriors must outpace a wildfire or run down an animal driven before the flames.

Crystalrock: Originally discovered by the dwarves of Janderhoff, who sometimes refer to it as the "Heart of the World," this massive crystalline formation hangs suspended from frail-looking crystal threads in a natural cavern far beneath the edge of the Mindspin Mountains. For hundreds of years, dwarven elders have gathered here annually to watch as the crystal suddenly convulses, sending out a deep, vibrating pulse that can be felt in creatures' bones for miles around. Recently, however, the dwarves who study Crystalrock have grown withdrawn with concern and excitement as the beating has begun speeding up, currently coinciding with the changing of the seasons.

Crystilan: While its original name has long been lost, the site called Crystilan is today among the best-known Thassilonian artifacts, and has provided scholars with much of what they now know about Thassilonian life. Visible from the sea, the shining dome of translucent crystal is glorious to behold, catching the sun's light and making it too bright to stare upon directly. Up close, the adventurous can peer through the smooth, almost frictionless crystal at the chunk of city within, perfectly preserved like a fly in amber. Though many have attempted to break through and reach the great stepped temples and vast arches, no magic or weapon currently known has ever been able to mar or otherwise penetrate the crystal, and those who have attempted to tunnel under it believe the strange shield to be a perfect sphere. For now, at least, most scholars are content to transcribe the visible runes and watch the strangely deserted city as it proceeds, unchanging, through the ages toward some unknown purpose.

Curchain Hills: The hollows and grassy dells of the Curchain Hills are home to relatively peaceful tribes of Shoanti, great herds of grazing aurochs, and several superstitious families of frontiersmen. Travelers through the region often claim that certain hills appear too similar, suggesting an unnatural formation.

Ember Lake: Presumably fed by hot springs as well as the Lampblack and Malgorian rivers, the waters of Ember Lake rise up warm from the rolling plains, certain spots along the shore steaming in the colder months. The lake is also home to strange aquatic creatures that dart like fireflies in massive schools beneath the surface. Not quite fish, these tiny creatures called "charigs" resemble salamanders, their transparent skin phosphorescing in the clear waters. Although the creatures appear harmless, locals avoid eating them, claiming that on certain nights of the year the schools assemble in flickering patterns miles wide, moving with purpose and intelligence, as if creating glowing signals visible only from the sky.

Fenwall Mountains: While few attempt to establish any real homesteads in the monster-infested Fenwall Mountains, the peaks' rich lodes of iron and precious metals make them an attractive destination for those lower-class and undesirable Korvosans seeking to strike it big as prospectors. As such, the valleys of the Fenwalls are dotted with tiny one-man camps as well as heavily guarded strip-mining excavations bankrolled by larger, Korvosa-based mining concerns.

Fogscar Mountains: The dense-packed goblins of the Fogscar Mountains squabble among themselves constantly, with each stony gully seeming to host a new tribe of knee-biting scavengers. Although narrow roads run between the misty peaks, travelers seeking a shortcut between Magnimar and Roderic's Cove are advised to go well-armed and carry large stores of cheap trinkets—or moderately useful garbage—with which to buy off the notoriously covetous natives.

The Gnashers: The traditional home of several hill giant tribes, the Gnashers offer the brave explorer a rare glimpse into the vast giant empire that preceded human settlement in Varisia. Unfortunately, the brutish natures of its current residents make such expeditions a dangerous gamble at best.

Gruankus: Its original purpose unknown, the great stone wheel of Gruankus lies on the shore of the Varisian Gulf, its rune-carved bulk half-buried in the sand. Today, it's better remembered as the site of the negotiations between Riddleport and Magnimarian diplomats that led to the Treaty of Gruankus, which has kept traders in the Varisian Gulf nominally safe from pirate attacks for nearly a hundred years.

Guiltspur: Even the giant savages that dominate the northern Storval Plateau avoid Guiltspur, an ever-deepening excavation into ages long past, dug by giant sweat and dragon claw. Unmarked and unknown for centuries, only the coming of the aged and accursed blue dragon Cadrilkasta revealed the site of a complex Thassilonian catacomb. Now, the dragon enslaves ogres and giants to sift through the buried layers of the seemingly endless sepulcher, ignoring the impotent ghosts of the ages in pursuit of some treasure known only to her.

Hollow Mountain: Upon the largest of Rivenrake Island's jagged peaks sneers the shattered, monumental visage of a stern-looking woman scowling ever south over the remnants of the titanic ancient bridge that connected Rivenrake to Argavist Island. Shorn vertically in two, the face's broken half reveals levels upon levels of exposed architecture within the mountain, while below, the ruined foundations of a dust-choked tomb of a city climb the mountainside, tempting adventurers with the promise of untold discoveries.

Hook Mountain: This massive peak, inhabited by savage tribes of inbred ogres, is detailed further in "The Hook Mountain Massacre."

Ilsurian: In the years immediately following the crumbling of the Chelaxian Empire, Korvosa was embroiled in turmoil, the various noble houses and government officials squabbling to decide where the colony's allegiance would fall. While many loyal to the old empire eventually left the city, relocating to Magnimar, theirs was not the only faction to desert the quarreling city. Ilsur, formerly a First Sword among the Knights of Aroden, advocated a shaking off of noble rule altogether and the restructuring of Korvosa as an efficient, military meritocracy. He campaigned for

DWARF HALFLING ELF HUMAN GNOME

years but conceded failure in 4631 AR with the foundation of the Korvosan royal house. Ilsur led his troops to the coast of Lake Syrantula, where they settled in a small fishing village and dug in to await their chance to return and put the new aristocracy to the sword. Although Ilsur is long dead and his descendants are more woodsmen and fishmongers than soldiers, the village remains fiercely independent—ceding to neither Korvosan nor Magnimarian rule—and all townsfolk are required to maintain a sharp sword and train against the day when they might have to defend their freedom from tyrants.

The Iron Peaks: Although the farms in the valleys along their southwestern edge benefit from the mountains' rain shadow, the Iron Peaks are renowned as the domain of easily irritated ogres, hill giants, and stone giants. Wherever possible, locals avoid venturing beyond the range's foothills, and advise travelers to do the same.

Janderhoff: With its massive iron curtain wall and steeples of beaten copper, the dwarven stronghold of Janderhoff squats like a great armored beast among the foothills of the Mindspin Mountains.

Yet, despite its forbidding appearance, the city is a bustling nexus of trade, with Shoanti and Chelaxians alike passing through the well-guarded tunnels that form the city's only entrances. Once inside, visitors quickly find themselves in the low-ceilinged markets and smithies that provide the city's livelihood. These surface buildings are mostly for receiving outsiders, as the majority of the town's population lives belowground in an intricate lattice of subterranean streets.

Kaer Maga: This anarchic cliff-top city is built inside the ruins of an ancient Thassilonian fortress. For more information, see page 72 and *GameMastery Module D2: Seven Swords of Sin.*

Kodar Mountains: Tall and forbidding, the jagged snow-capped peaks of the Kodar Mountains are among the highest in the world. Only the hardiest creatures, such as storm giants, rocs, and several dragons, are able to withstand the extreme climate and treacherous cliffs. Numerous mysteries and legends have origins hidden deep within the Kodar Mountains, such as the quixotic Monastery of the Peacock Spirit, the cloud citadel of Chadra-Oon, and the lost city of Xin-Shalast.

HALF-ORC   HALF-ELF

RACES OF VARISIA

Humans are by far the most common race in Varisia, and generally fall into one of three ethnicities—the cultured Chelaxians of the cities, the nomadic Varisians, or the fiercely tribal Shoanti barbarians. The elves, recently returned from an age-long absence, are far taller and thinner than humans, with long pointed ears and pupils so large they fill much of the eye. Most elves keep to their own kind, preferring the wild places where, over time, they take on aspects of their environment. Occasionally a traveler in Varisia might run into one of the Forlorn—lonely elves who grew up in non-elf lands among folk who are born and die in the time it takes an elf to reach maturity.

Dwarves in Varisia are stocky miners and stalwart fighters, generally concentrated around their stronghold of Janderhoff. Halflings, in contrast, are nomadic and have no set homeland, preferring instead to latch onto other races and wedge themselves into the cracks in any given society. Gnomes are by far the most mysterious and magical of the civilized races, and their vibrantly colored hair and skin show the influence of nature and their fey roots. While gnomes are generally no more evil than the other races, their alien thought processes and adherence to an unconventional moral code tend to make other races uneasy.

Half-breeds such as half-elves and half-orcs are exceedingly rare in Varisia, though this should not stop a player from running one of them as a character. Half-elves, with their extended lifespan, face many of the same problems and prejudices as the Forlorn, while half-orcs are almost universally mistrusted by all but their orc brethren. (True orcs, for their part, frequently conduct raids into human lands specifically to breed more half-orcs, as the smarter half-breeds make the best leaders of the various orc tribes.)

For a more detailed overview of the races of Varisia, consult the *Rise of the Runelords Player's Guide*.

The Lady's Light: Leaning precariously at the end of a rocky spit, the Lady's Light is a southern sailor's first glimpse of Varisia. Nearly two hundred feet high, the enormous stone lighthouse is shaped like a sensuous woman in a flowing dress that leaves one breast bare, her right hand pointing a staff that shines a brilliant beam of light out to sea at regular intervals. At the statue's base, a gigantic, strangely hinged stone door presumably leads into the lighthouse's interior, but none are known to have unlocked it in modern times.

Lake Skotha: This lake is considered holy by the local hill giants, who refuse to visit it except during funerals. Whenever one of their number dies, he is placed on a barge that is then set aflame and pushed out onto the water, that his spirit might join his ancestors on the mysterious central island. The giants don't take kindly to outsiders, but those who enter the lake find its bottom coated in a thick layer of giant bones.

Lake Stormunder: Lake Stormunder takes its name from the extensive underwater geysers that boil and churn in its depths. On its shores, fishermen are sometimes forced to take shelter as rocs skim low over the surface looking for prey. For more information, see *Pathfinder #5*.

Lake Syrantula: One of the most frequently traveled waterways in Varisia, this hundred-mile-long lake is a primary part of the trade route between Korvosan and Magnimarian holdings. Though most of the fishermen and sailors who ply its waters have little more to fear than the giant gars that are a major food source for nearby communities, none can truly say what beasts might slumber in such an enormous body of water, and most of those who live along its shores are careful to avoid the mysterious ruins that dot its southern border.

Lurkwood: Once the home of countless elves, the Lurkwood is now staunchly avoided by its one-time protectors for reasons they refuse to name. Locals whisper that the forest has come loose from the march of years, and stories circulate of travelers who wandered into it, only to emerge far younger or older than they ought to be. One thing's for certain—the seasons in Lurkwood don't appear to correspond to those of the land around it, its leaves changing colors and falling even while farmers' fields are new and green.

Malgorian Mountains: While adventurous herdsmen make this one of the most civilized mountain ranges in Varisia, it's also one of the most geologically active. Although it contains few volcanoes of any real size, geysers, hot springs, and bubbling tar pits dot the range, filling the mountains with strange and sometimes choking clouds and making travel treacherous for those unused to such hazards. Though close-mouthed about such things to other races, the gnomes of Sanos Forest seem particularly taken with these geologic features, and troops of the little folk can sometimes be found ringing a geyser long after sunset, performing some sort of private prayer or ritual.

Mierani Forest: The regional home of the elves since time immemorial, the Mierani Forest is a place of enormous, spreading trees and abundant wildlife. The Mierani elves maintain the forest as a civilized wilderness, allowing the course of nature to run unimpeded and protecting it from monstrous threats and axe-wielding interlopers. While small elven communities guard the wooded fringe and wandering feral-born patrol the depths, the elves are still in the process of cleansing the forest after their centuries-long absence, their most persistent quarries being tribes of ettercaps, ravenous plants, and a singularly elusive green dragon known as Razorhorn.

Minderhal's Anvil: This ancient temple-mountain rises in honor of Minderhal, the brooding smith-god of the giants. Beyond its cracking marble pillars, the massive forge-altar still stands, its cold furnace once fed with the bodies of convicted lawbreakers. Few giants now come here, and the stone statue of the giant lord of judgment sits unattended on his throne, chin resting on his fist, staring out across the Storval Deep.

Mindspin Mountains: Filled with giants, ogres, and trolls, not to mention deep crevasses and dangerous rockslides, the Mindspin Mountains are considered a deathtrap for all but the most experienced travelers. Ironically, such dangers might be one of Varisia's greatest assets, as to date they've kept the warring orc tribes of the Hold of Belkzen from sweeping across the range into Korvosa.

The Mobhad Leigh: With a Shoanti name meaning "steps into hell," the Mobhad Leigh has captivated imaginations for ages. A perfectly round pit in an otherwise nondescript field at the foot of the Kodar Mountains, the Leigh has so far never been conclusively proved to have a bottom. Steps spiraling along the pit's sheer walls extend down for several hundred feet before collapsing, and those who have ventured farther have never returned to say whether or not they begin again lower down. The local Shoanti generally avoid the Leigh, particularly after several of their magic-users dropped dead while attempting to scout the pit with scrying magic. Yet on certain nights of the year, flickering orange lights can be seen dancing deep within its depths.

Mundatei: The Obelisk Forest of Mundatei is no true forest. Rather, when passing over the ridge into Mundatei's wide valley, the traveler's first impression is of a vast tangle of menhirs—thousands upon thousands of ten-foot-high stones carved in places with spiraling patterns of runes. It's a breathtaking display, and rumor has long held that some of the obelisks are hollow and contain treasures.

But when a group of Korvosan explorers broke open a dozen of the obelisks nearly a hundred years ago, they found that each obelisk contained a twisted, long-dead human body, its limbs and expression frozen in pain and horror. That evening, the explorers' camps were assaulted by horrific undead whose flesh was hard as stone and whose eyes were horribly alive and fresh. A dozen folk were carried off by the undead, and when the survivors searched for them the next day no trace was found—but the twelve opened obelisks had reformed into their previous shapes as if they had never been touched. Few have returned to Mundatei since that fateful day.

The Mushfens: South of the Yondabakari, the land becomes a sweating tangle of boggy marshes and impenetrable mangroves, endless meres and fens capable of swallowing men without a trace. Along with the usual dangers of the swamp, the Mushfens are known for their vicious populations of boggards, marsh giants, and faceless stalkers. (For more information, see *Pathfinder #2* and *Pathfinder #5*.)

The Nolands: The Nolands are rough, stony plains where the tribes of the Linnorm Kings exile their most despicable and craven criminals. Centuries of this practice has given rise to numerous bands of berserkers who roam the land, preying upon each other, slaughtering without mercy, and feasting on the flesh of their enemies. While the Nolanders are too disorganized to prove any real threat to Varisia, residents of the Velashu Uplands and Red Mountains are constantly on guard against the savage raids of the northerners. Some Shoanti tribes banish their criminals to the Nolands as well, although such a punishment is generally seen as less honorable than a clean death.

Ravenmoor: Quaint and isolated, the residents of Ravenmoor are happy to trade with those passing through along the Lampblack River, but travelers seeking to spend the night find that none of the empty-looking inns accept boarders. Additionally, while apparently extremely pious, the residents are loath to discuss their religious beliefs with outsiders.

Red Mountains: The Red Mountains are relatively low by Varisian standards, their rocky soil rusted red with thick iron deposits. The residents, primarily miners and herdsmen, eke out meager livings from the barren hills, banding together on their shaggy upland ponies against the lawless raiders of the Nolands. So close to the berserkers, the ridges and gullies of the Red Mountains hold a natural appeal for paladins and rangers, who make it their calling to protect Varisia's northern border. Of late, the raiders appear disturbingly organized, and many of the local leaders have begun appealing to the southlands for aid, even going so far as to send emissaries to Riddleport and the Hellknights stationed in Magnimar.

Riddleport: Varisia's northernmost port, the infamous city of Riddleport is renowned as a haven for scoundrels, outcasts, and worse. Cutthroats fill its harbor and dockside brothels, with Riddleport's officers of the law being just another gang of thieves (and hardly the most powerful one at that). Yet even in such a den of inequity and vice, scholars and historians abound, attempting to decipher the runes of the great arch known as the Cyphergate, which spans the mouth of the harbor and looms over each vessel that passes into the city. Although any progress on the inscription has been kept quiet, recent excavation hints that the massive arch might actually be just one segment of a ring that extends into the cliffs surrounding the port.

Rift of Niltak: Whether the Rift of Niltak was opened by great magic or some geologic calamity, none alive today can say. Filled with strange, pulsing structures and bizarre flora, the canyon's mist-shrouded depths swarm with enormous centipede-like horrors, shrieking bat-like predators, and worse. It should be noted that accurate descriptions of the depths are made that much rarer by the high suicide rate among the few explorers who return from journeys below.

Rimeskull: From where they stand, high on the mountain's steep western slopes and staring out toward Lake Stormunder, the strange, heavy stone statues of Rimeskull—each a massive head of eroded rock—have puzzled scholars for ages. Who made them, and why they all stare fixedly west, remains a mystery, due in no small part to the white dragon Arkrhyst, who makes Rimeskull his home and is notoriously disinclined to allow guests.

Roderic's Cove: Besieged by the goblins and bandits of Churlwood on one side and pirates on the other, the port-town of Roderic's Cove submitted to Riddleport 10 years ago. To everyone's surprise, both in the town and throughout Varisia, the pirates spared the community, employing it as a shipping and trading port for merchants without the stomach to enter Riddleport. Captain Jess Gildersleeve serves as port-governor, guaranteeing that the gangs of Riddleport get their cut of the local trade while assuring her own sizable take. In the wake of a recent rash of mysteriously scuttled ships in the harbor, many citizens who remember life before the pirates' rule have chalked the sabotage up to the ghost of Sir Roderic, the town's founder and a notorious privateer, while those in power blame rebellion and insurgents. With tensions rising, many believe it's only a matter of time before the battle lines are drawn and Roderic's Cove erupts in flames of revolution.

Sanos Forest: While Whistledown is regarded by other races as the primary gnome settlement in Varisia, Sanos Forest is their true domain. Here, under sun-dappled branches bowed low with moss and fungus, the gnomes prune and twist the living plants into elaborate dwellings. Here, too, they're free to drop the masks worn among other sentient races and revel in their true natures, organizing themselves along principles unknown to outsiders. Although gnomes as a race are extremely tight-lipped about what goes on in Sanos Forest, there are whispers that somewhere deep in its heart they maintain a gateway to the First World of the fey.

Shimmerglens: This reputedly haunted patch of swampland is detailed further in "The Hook Mountain Massacre."

Skull's Crossing: This immense Thassilonian dam is detailed further in "The Hook Mountain Massacre."

Spindlehorn: Thousands of feet high, Spindlehorn thrusts up from the shore of the Storval Deep like a needle against the sky, its sides sheer except for the treacherous set of stairs that winds around the crooked spire until it reaches the flattened peak, an open space barely 10 feet in diameter. None know what purpose

VARISIAN TRADITIONS

Varisia's native wanderers are well known as passionate people possessed of ancient talents, uncanny insight, and a mysterious connection to things unseen. Those who spend time among the Varisians are sure to witness, and perhaps participate in, a variety of their mystical traditions.

Dancing: For Varisians, dancing is a form of communication, and every dance has a meaning. Two dances are particularly important to the wanderers. In the well-known Trastaturi, or "Dance of Friends," young members energetically welcome visitors and offer the clan's hospitality. Conversely, the lesser known Vimaturi is never performed before non-Varisians. In this secretive "Dance of the Departed," the elders of the clan dance with their ancestors, calling upon the dead to guide and protect their families. It is said that any outsider who intrudes upon the Vimaturi will forever be haunted by the spirits of lost Varisians and never again know peace.

Fortunetelling: Despite the inaccuracy of magical foresight in the Age of Lost Omens, Varisians still practice their ancient fortunetelling traditions. Varisian seers most commonly divine the future through astrology, crystallomancy, cartomancy—employing elaborate, mystical cards known as a harrow deck—and face-reading. While many consider such divinations to be little more than vagaries and stage magic, aged Varisians—especially women—are widely respected and feared for their strange understanding of fortune and fate.

Tattooing: Varisians have a natural connection to magic, and many sorcerers arise from among the wanderers. Such nomadic magic-users often seek to empower their inner magic with external symbols of arcane might, scribing their bodies with any of seven elaborate arcane tattoos, each related to a separate school of magic (see the *Rise of the Runelords Player's Guide* for more details). The names of these arcane symbols are as follows:

Avaria: Transmutation

Avidais: Abjuration

Carnasia: Enchantment

Idolis: Conjuration

Ragario: Evocation

Vangloris: Illusion

Voratalo: Necromancy

the mysterious spire once served, but tales tell of dark-robed pilgrims seen climbing the dizzying stairs but never descending.

Spire of Lemriss: Not exactly a tree, the Spire of Lemriss is an enormous spike of plant matter stretching hundreds of feet into the sky, its near-vertical sides covered in an arm-deep shell of vines and its inner structure made of twisted and braided wooden trunks sprouting from each other in an endless cascade. Within its branches, birds and rodents nest and breed, their hoots echoed from the nearby Churlwood, along with the occasional screeching of something far larger. While some believe the spire to be a sprouted cutting from the World Tree, its true origins remain unknown.

Stony Mountains: While one of the few relatively giant-free mountain ranges in Varisia—kept that way by the warlike Shoanti of the Tamiir-Quah—the Stony Mountains are still dangerous for the unwary, as griffons, manticores, tribes of harpies, and other dangerous creatures make the craggy peaks their home.

The Storval Deep: Filling the entire valley between the Iron Peaks and the Wyvern Mountains, the Storval Deep is a massive lake held back by an ancient dam, Skull's Crossing, at its southern tip. What's more, the banks of the lake themselves seem curiously worked, as if carved from the surrounding stone by more than water. Although rumors abound of sunken cities, flooded mineshafts, and relics so powerful the ancients created the lake just to hide them, few have ever ventured into the dark water's unfathomed depths.

Storval Plateau: The land of Varisia is split in half by the Storval Rise, a thousand-foot-tall cliff sculpted for much of its length into ancient weatherworn statues, cliff fortresses, and strange portals into eldritch depths. The Rise separates the lush, fertile lowlands from the harsh, arid lands of the eastern plateau. Here, giants and tribes of hard-edged Shoanti hold sway, scratching an existence from the plateau hardpan or chasing herds of thundering aurochs across the sparse grasslands.

The Storval Stairs: Although sized for a colossus, the Storval Stairs are still the most expedient route from Varisia's western lowlands onto the plateau. Here, where the Storval Rise shrinks to only a few hundred feet of vertical cliff face, great stairs have been cut from the cliff, flanked on either side by enormous statues. In the thousands of years since the stairs' sculpting, lesser engineers have cut more convenient, human-sized steps and ramps into their sides, routes capable of handling entire platoons of explorers and adventurers.

The Sunken Queen: Slowly sinking into the waters of the swamp, this enormous stone pyramid is still imposing, with one entire side carved in a bas-relief of a beautiful naked woman. From the pyramid's peak extend numerous curving towers at strange angles, like growths or chimneys, and legends hold that within the Sunken Queen's austere walls lie layer upon layer of deadly catacombs filled with the secrets of the lost Thassilonian empire.

Turtleback Ferry: This remote settlement is detailed in "The Hook Mountain Massacre."

Urglin: The broken towers of Urglin rise like a sore from the blasted plain of the Cinderlands. Once the site of an ancient city, orcs from the Hold of Belkzen have plundered and ruined anything of value through decades of squatting and abuse, building over the ruined foundations with ramshackle ghettoes of scavenged rock, iron, and bone. Outcast Shoanti, giants, half-breeds, and other monstrosities roam the treacherous streets where strength is the only law. Through the center of the city, giving it life, flows the sluggish Ooze, a stream polluted to the consistency of pudding by the city's waste.

Varisian Gulf: When the Thassilonian Empire shattered ten thousand years ago, much of western Varisia fell into the sea, becoming what is now known as the Varisian Gulf. Although only Hollow Mountain and a few remnants of Magnimar's great Irespan remain as reminders of nations lost to the waves, those salvagers who earn their living exploring the sea bottom here find it surprisingly rife with ruined cities and ancient relics of extraordinary size.

Velashu Uplands: The horse lords of the Velashu Uplands are widely regarded as the best horse breeders in Varisia. Astride their great destriers, the Velashans race across their domain, thanklessly protecting the southern lands and occasionally venturing to Riddleport or beyond to charge top price for their magnificent steeds.

Viperwall: Embossed with great stone serpents, the conical roofs of this brooding castle's many towers shine in the moonlight. Avoided by locals, the structure is often surrounded by a greenish haze of poisonous gas which leaks steadily from fanged sculptures in its walls.

Whistledown: Named for the distinctive wooden charms that hang from house eaves to turn the evening wind off the lake into haunting melodies, Whistledown lies at the western tip of the Fenwall Mountains, where Lake Syrantula becomes the Yondabakari once more. Although the town is home to almost as many humans as gnomes, Whistledown is generally regarded as the primary gnome settlement in Varisia, and most of the quaint white-walled cottages are sized accordingly. Although the town has a reputation as a peaceful, friendly trade stop, most non-gnome visitors find the town's nightly serenade disturbing in ways they can't quite explain.

Windsong Abbey: Established by pacifist, scholarly monks as a forum for interfaith discussion, the vast sandstone edifice of Windsong Abbey emerges from the seaside cliffs in sweeping arches and towers, stained glass windows catching the light and tunnels in its walls and foundation channeling the wind into music like that of a pipe organ. Although at one time clergy from all of Varisia's major religions—both good and evil—met here to resolve conflicts and diplomatically further the goals of their various deities, since Aroden's death several churches have withdrawn from the assembly, disregarding years of cooperation and collected prophecy. Although the abbey is an impressive architectural feat in its own right, the Masked Abbess and her closest advisors know it's actually built atop the ruins of a much older structure.

Wormwood Hall: Overgrown with creeping vines, this large manor house deep within the Lurkwood squats forebodingly, its windows dark and lintels covered with strange, twisting runes. While none in recent memory have ventured inside, many believe that Wormwood Hall is somehow tied to the forest's unnatural seasons.

Wyvern Mountains: This range's name says it all, and travelers here are advised to keep a sharp eye out for roving packs of the poisonous draconic predators that subsist on the mountains' wild goats and free-roaming llamas.

MAGNIMARIAN HOLDINGS

The city of Magnimar is slowly bringing nearby settlements under its governance, setting itself up to become the capital of a fledgling nation.

Galduria: While the town of Galduria survives primarily by ferrying grain and lumber along the Lampblack River and Ember Lake, its true claim to fame is its college. By far the oldest structure in town, the Twilight Academy is one of the premier schools of magic in Varisia, rivaled only by the Stone of the Seers in Magnimar and the notorious Acadamae of Korvosa, both of which consider it an upstart devoid of their own rich heritages. Founded in Galduria specifically to avoid the political pressure and intrigues of those two cities, the Twilight Academy has a reputation as being experimental and unconventional in many of its practices, but frequent donations to public works keep locals from probing too deeply into the occasional haywire spell or necromantic accident.

Magnimar: Founded by former Korvosans seeking to throw off Chelish rule and form a democratic metropolis, the renowned City of Monuments lies at the southern tip of the Varisian Gulf, built up around one of the last surviving remnants of the enormous bridge that purportedly once stretched all the way to Hollow Mountain. One of the two major powers vying for control of Varisia, Magnimar is detailed extensively in *Pathfinder #2*.

Nybor: Renowned for its racial tolerance, this peaceful farming community has a greater number of half-breeds per capita than anywhere else in Varisia, and strongly encourages interracial marriages. While it occasionally draws the ire of puritan sects, many are the young Magnimarian noblewomen who are quietly bundled up and shipped off to Nybor when an illicit fling results in pregnancy.

Sandpoint: Sandpoint is a sleepy fishing town known primarily for its excellent theater and exquisite glassblowing, and the only settlement of note on the Lost Coast. Of late, the town has been experiencing an unusual spate of murders and goblin troubles. For more information, see *Pathfinder #1*.

Wartle: A ramshackle trading post full of swampers and fur traders, Wartle perches on stilts above the muck of the Mushfens. For more information, see *Pathfinder #2*.

Wolf's Ear: At one time, Wolf's Ear was the lycanthrope version of a leper colony, where werewolves and other such persecuted humanoids could live together in relative safety and comfort. When the town was annexed by Magnimar, however, the Lord-Mayor decided that such things were indecent and bankrolled a pogrom by the Church of Erastil designed to "cleanse" the town. In the ensuing bloody fracas, the lycanthropes were driven underground, where the Magnimarian leaders, unprepared for such passionate resistance, were content to let them stay. The official Magnimarian position is that any rumors of lycanthropy are just that, and those pointing out the townsfolk's unusual habits are quickly coerced into silence.

ENCOUNTERS IN VARISIA

Travelers might come upon any number of threats and strange sights as they wander Varisia's unforgiving wilds.

Animals: A variety of unique creatures are native to Varisia's wildly contrasting environments. Many of these have the same stats as similar creatures, as detailed below.

Aurochs: Advanced 7 HD bison

Alligator: Crocodile

Nightbelly Boa: Giant constrictor snake

Ember Scorpion: Large monstrous scorpion

Firepelt Cougar: Leopard

Redback Rattlesnake: Large viper

Great White Shark: Huge Shark

Brigands: Numerous criminals prey upon unwary travelers in Varisia. Simple roadside brigands, Riddleport pirates, raiders from the Hold of Belkzen, Nolander barbarians, and worse all might see PCs as easy marks. A brigand encounter usually has an EL within two steps of the PCs' level.

Dragon: Although rare, several dragons make their homes throughout Varisia. PCs are most likely to encounter an adult dragon of a color appropriate to the surrounding terrain.

Flame Drakes: These fire-breathing dragonkin inhabit Bloodsworn Vale to the southeast of Varisia. See *GameMastery Module W1: Conquest of Bloodsworn Vale* for more details.

Patrol: Patrols are wandering groups aligned with the dominant powers of a specific area, ranging in form and strength depending upon where they are encountered. Korvosan guards, Shoanti hunters, the Whistledown militia, or Varisian wanderers could all cross paths with PCs traveling in their areas of influence. While not necessarily combat encounters, patrols have ELs appropriate to their form. Thus, a band of Baslwief merchants might only be EL 2, while a patrol of hellknights might be EL 8 or higher.

KORVOSAN HOLDINGS

The first Varisian colony established by the Chelaxian Empire, Korvosa still retains nominal control over several nearby townships in an attempt to preserve some of its former glory.

Abken: The town of Abken was founded on a belief: that given the right blend of people, a town might work as a single family, with no one man better than any other. Originally just a few families from the Korvosan underclass, this simple farming commune grew slowly, with new members admitted only through marriage or majority vote. Although friendly to strangers, the now-sizeable village remains insular and tight-lipped about its internal processes, the large log palisade around the primary compound protecting its privacy. Outsiders causing trouble can expect to be subdued in short order, as every man, woman, and child is quick to raise arms in defense of their "family."

Biston: Here the shores of Lake Syrantula rise up from the water in a great overhanging cliff of stone. Covering the escarpment is an ancient and crumbling community, its caves drilled back into the rock to form a cozy, interconnected warren of ladders and ropes. Although the town is currently inhabited primarily by fishermen and farmers, its original architects are rumored to have been a now-extinct tribe of harpies.

Baslwief: Baslwief is one of the primary mining towns in the Korvosan region, its residents prying iron, copper, and rarer metals from the foothills of the Fenwall Mountains and shipping them downriver. In addition to human prospectors, the town boasts a large population of halflings, who find the city's frontier aesthetic much to their liking.

Korvosa: Formerly the capital of colonial Varisia, Korvosa suffered several years of turmoil after the fall of the Chelaxian Empire, and emerged from this struggle roughly equivalent with Magnimar in terms of political power—a fact that still irks many of Korvosa's residents. These days, most of Korvosa's decadent nobles continue to play up their ties to Cheliax and their endorsement of southern fashions, fancying themselves Varisia's center of culture and enlightenment. Whether or not such conceits are accurate, the city is certainly tied the closest to the land's imperial past.

Harse: This village perches on the spit of land where the Sarwin and Falcon Rivers meet, and the twin Harse Ferries are the easiest way for travelers in the area to cross either of the great rivers. In addition, Harse boasts the best horse and livestock breeders south of the Velashu Uplands, and each year holds an enormous rodeo designed to single out the best animals and riders.

Melfesh: The town of Melfesh stretches across the Yondabakari on long piers, the river's current turning the numerous great waterwheels that power their grain and lumber mills. A vast drawbridge at the town's center raises and lowers, allowing the town to levy a toll from any ship or caravan wishing to pass—a practice that earns no love from the captains who trade on this stretch of the river.

Palin's Cove: Here the clear waters of the Falcon River turn brown and black as the factories of Palin's Cove, Korvosa's industrial center, vent waste material into its current. A relatively recent development, the factories have drawn great animosity and even violence from druids, Gozreh worshipers, and even ordinary smiths and craftsmen, but none can deny that the quality of the goods turned out by these workhouses provides a huge boost to the Korvosan economy.

Sirathu: This hamlet is both the poorest and farthest removed of Korvosa's holdings. Although generally dismissed by their "leaders" to the south as filthy peasants, the folk of Sirathu have recently come to the city's notice by rallying behind a 10-year-old child who reportedly predicts the future and urges secession from the corruption of Korvosa "before the storm breaks."

Veldraine: Known as the "Gateway to Korvosa," Veldraine is an important trade port and a key military position, given its placement at the mouth of Conquerer's Bay. In addition to housing much of the Korvosan Navy and vast amounts of artillery, the town of Veldraine is also equipped with an enormous winch capable of raising an immense chain off the sea floor and stretching it taut across the bay's narrow mouth, sealing Korvosa off from the ocean and potentially stranding attackers in the bay, where they can easily be picked off.

WANDERING MONSTERS IN VARISIA

Much of Varisia remains untamed and dangerous. Here are but a few of the most common threats travelers might face when wandering these wild lands.

Forest	Lowland	Mountain	Plateau	Swamp	Aquatic	Monster	Avg. EL	Source
—	—	01–09	01–10	01–04	—	1 giant gecko	1	*Pathfinder #1*
01–04	—	—	—	05–09	—	1 goblin snake	1	*Pathfinder #1*
05–12	01–05	10–17	—	—	—	1d2 firepelt cougars*	2	MM
—	06–08	18–23	11–15	—	—	1 redback rattlesnake*	2	MM
—	—	—	—	10–22	—	1d4 alligators*	2	MM
13–22	09–18	—	—	23–31	—	2d6 goblins	3	MM
23	—	—	—	—	—	1 dryad	3	MM
—	—	—	16–20	—	—	1 ember scorpion*	3	MM
—	—	—	—	—	01–07	1 bunyip	3	*Tome of Horrors*
24–31	—	—	—	—	—	1 owlbear	4	MM
—	19–23	—	—	—	—	1d6 ghouls	4	MM
32–41	24–33	—	—	32–44	—	2d6 stirges	4	MM
—	—	—	—	—	08–20	1 great white shark*	4	MM
42–46	—	—	—	—	—	1 dire boar	4	MM
—	—	—	21–30	—	—	2d6 orcs	5	MM
47–50	34–37	24–27	31–35	—	—	1 manticore	5	MM
51–56	—	—	—	45–52	—	1 nightbelly boa*	5	MM
57–60	—	28–31	36–38	53–57	—	1 troll	5	MM
—	—	32–36	39–44	—	21–30	1d2 giant eagles	5	MM
—	—	—	—	—	31–45	1 orca whale	5	MM
—	—	—	—	58–67	—	1d6 boggards	6	*Pathfinder #2*
—	—	—	—	68–71	—	1 will-o'-wisp	6	MM
61–69	38–47	37–44	—	—	—	2d8 wolves	6	MM
—	48–55	45–49	45–52	—	—	1d6 ogres	7	MM
70–74	56–60	50–56	—	72–76	—	1d4 harpies	7	MM
—	—	—	—	77–84	46–54	1d4 scrags	7	MM
—	61	—	53–54	—	—	1 bulette	7	MM
75–80	—	57–61	—	—	—	1 dire bear	7	MM
—	62–63	62–65	55–57	—	—	1d4 gargoyles	7	MM
81–83	—	—	—	85–86	—	1d4 flame drakes	8	See page 69
—	—	66–67	—	—	55–56	1 roc	9	MM
—	—	68–70	58–61	—	57–61	1d4 wyverns	9	MM
—	—	—	—	—	62–68	1 giant squid	9	MM
—	—	—	—	—	69–75	1 dire shark	9	MM
—	64–71	—	62–75	—	—	3d10 aurochs*	10	MM
—	—	71–80	76–78	—	—	1d4 stone giants	11	MM
—	72–76	81–87	79–85	—	—	1d4 hill giants	11	MM
—	—	—	—	87–92	—	1d6 marsh giants	12	*Pathfinder #5*
—	—	88–90	—	—	—	1d6 tagia giants	14	*Pathfinder #4*
84–90	77–92	91–95	86–95	93–95	76–90	Patrol	Variable	See page 69
91–99	93–99	96–99	96–99	96–99	91–99	Brigands	Variable	See page 69
100	100	100	100	100	100	Dragon	Variable	See page 69

* Each of these creatures is analogous to an animal in the MM. See page 70 for specific details.

HAND OF THE HANDLESS

2 Desnus, 4707 AR

Standing at the foot of the Storval Rise is like looking into the face of a god—sometimes literally, as in places the rocks have been hewn into massive representations of kings and demagogues whose identities are long lost to memory. The point where Kaer Maga breaks the relentless trudge of the plateau is no exception. Even as I write this, the city leers down at me from its perch, a thousand feet of vertical cliff face separating us. Waterfalls from the city's underground aquifers cascade down among graven images and portals into the fabled dungeons honeycombing the rock beneath the city, joined by long streaks of a less pleasant nature—I suppose when your window overlooks a chasm, the motivation to walk elsewhere to empty your chamber pot grows less and less.

While most trade caravans follow the Yondabakari all the way to the pass a few miles southeast, taking the easier ascent and following the ridgeline to the city, I decided to take what I find the more romantic approach: the Twisted Door. While most of the dungeons beneath Kaer Maga remain unexplored and viewed—correctly—as dangerous by the locals, there is one notable exception. From a set of huge bronze double-doors at the base of the cliff, the Halflight Path rises up through the rock, occasionally emerging to wind in treacherous goat paths along the exposed cliff face before plunging back into the stone. Vital to the city's trade efforts, this particular path is kept clear by the Duskwardens, a devoted group of almost monastic guardians who see through merchants and other travelers and keep horrors from the rest of the catacombs from invading the passage. All for a modest fee, of course.

Tomorrow morning I'll make my ascent and begin looking for Dakar, but for now, the sunset over the lowlands demands my full attention.

3 Desnus, 4707 AR

Sweet Desna, that was a lot of stairs. I need a drink.

3 Desnus, 4707 AR
Evening

Please excuse the wax drippings on this page—the owner of the Sorry Excuse charges extra for lighted rooms, and I'm already paying an arm and a leg for the use of this hacked-up desk. I shudder to think what the bargain rooms must be like, though judging from the commotion in the common room below, most of the patrons will be in little condition to pass judgment. But I digress.

I awoke at dawn this morning and joined the already growing line of merchants and travelers forming in front of the Twisted Door. Up close, the gates are even more impressive—the gleaming bronze is covered in embossed runes. Moreover, the doors themselves, which appear straight from a distance, are actually subtly warped, their edges seeming to rotate at strange angles, yet still fitting together without a gap. Running your eyes along any particular line, it's perfectly straight, yet when you reach its end you find that your vision has somehow curved, like the toymaker's twisted rings that have only one side. Truly curious.

Shortly after my arrival, the doors swung open and disgorged a dozen armed men garbed in dusty browns and grays, each bearing a badge on his right breast depicting a gold arch against a midnight blue background. These, then, were the Duskwardens. With an efficiency born of repetition, the bored-looking men levied their fee—a not-insignificant sum—from each trader and wanderer before organizing those assembled into small groups, which they then led into the gaping tunnel at intervals, each headed by one of the wiry, stern-faced men. The warden assigned to my group was named Darien, and when queried, he explained that the gaps between groups were intended to help the Duskwardens keep order, give them room to fight if necessary, and keep the travelers from proving too tempting a target for the dark things that hunt beneath Kaer Maga.

After a short wait we set off into the tunnel, the wardens loaning small glowing pendants to those in need of light. The path began to rise almost immediately, and though the way curved and doubled back enough to remain feasible for the merchants' horses and carts, before long the muscles in my legs burned like hot wires. Our guide, for his part, moved nimbly before us and between us, not quite dancing circles around us, but constantly ensuring that the darkness beyond our meager illumination held no surprises. Though the wardens sweep the tunnels constantly for danger, the threat was not so distant that we could afford to be careless. At

GOING DEEPER

While most of its residents are content to live in the city's soaring towers and hollow walls, Kaer Maga's surface structures are just the tip of the iceberg. Beneath the bustling markets, an intricate network of dungeons, tunnels, and complexes extends down through the Storval Ridge, and perhaps even farther. Although the top few levels have been frequently inhabited and remodeled by various daring organizations, incursions by the dangerous creatures that inhabit the lower reaches led the city to establish the Duskwardens, charged with seeking out and sealing all entrances to the greater catacombs. Even so, the depths of Kaer Maga remain uncharted and hold a powerful allure for foolhardy adventurers.

GameMastery Module D2: Seven Swords of Sin offers additional background on Kaer Maga, sending PCs into a well-defended arcane stronghold beneath the city in order to stop a powerful sorceress from awakening relics dating back to the time of the Runelords themselves.

several points we passed side-tunnels that had been bricked up, and in these places Darien instructed us to move as quietly as possible lest we attract the attention of creatures that might view the bricks as mere inconveniences. At one such wall I paused, and from beyond it I heard the faint sounds of roaring, a deep bellow that made the rock buzz, combined with a high squealing that cut off sharply. From that point on, the merchants and I found renewed strength to quicken our pace.

The path itself is an architectural hodgepodge. At its base it's hewn primarily from the raw stone, following natural seams and tunnels, but at several points it changes drastically, at one point becoming a tube so smooth that only the sand spread on the floor keeps the foot from slipping, while at another suddenly displaying ornate masonry and elaborate frescoes. Once, we seemed to actually be walking down a hallway in some grand subterranean city, the doors flanking us barred with locks and chains. The most harrowing portions of the journey, however, were those in which the tunnel emerged onto the cliff-face, becoming a ledge just wide enough for a cart, before plunging back into the rock. The view was magnificent, but one look over the edge at the sheer drop below us was enough for me, and I spent the rest of these spans hugging the wall.

Finally, however, the tunnel disgorged us into a small stone-walled corral on the plateau's surface, just a stone's throw from the walls of the city. Darien collected our pendants, thanked us brusquely, and loped back into the tunnel's mouth, scarcely winded.

Over half a mile in diameter, Kaer Maga's hexagonal ring of eighty-foot-high walls looms stark and imposing. The numerous doors and windows the residents have chiseled out at every height hold anchors for ropes and baskets, wooden ladders, or vast nets like the rigging on a ship. Up these precarious routes men and women climb without hesitation, the children scampering fearlessly from landing to landing, to pass through the haphazard portals into homes or thoroughfares. For where any other city might have a curtain wall,

Then it stood, drew a knife from a hidden fold in its garment, and before I could move, thrust it into its own belly.

Kaer Maga is its walls—a solid ring hundreds of feet thick, hosting chambers large enough to house entire districts, many of them stacked one on top of the other.

For the outsider, though, the most common road into the city is through the Warren, and it was there that I found myself. Just as no one knows Kaer Maga's original purpose before generations of squatters turned its mysterious chambers into a bustling city, no one today knows what cataclysm might have breached these walls, though several theories reflect the fact that citizens born in the Warren seem subtly twisted, their women more likely to miscarry. Where the huge stones of the Ring end, blasted away to reveal the layered chambers inside, a new structure rises up to bridge the gap: a precarious shantytown of scrap lumber and broken stone. Here, in the Warren, a maze of scaffolding as high as the surrounding walls hides the city's poorest citizens, a vertical slum where bare planks create a maze that threatens to swallow the unwary. Through this the main road passes with no gates or guards—simply seven stories of staring eyes and grasping hands. The latter I managed to bat away, staring down the would-be guides that descended like flies as I moved through their muddy streets and into the open-air city center that locals call the Core.

For most travelers, the journey into Kaer Maga stops at the Core. The only places in the city to receive regular sunlight, the three districts of the Core are considered neutral ground by the loose alliance of gangs and guilds that rule the city in an anarchic, mercenary, and utterly tribal fashion. To the north, Widdershins provides relatively posh housing for those with means, and to the south Downmarket and Hospice milk gold from locals and transients alike through trade and lodging. In the middle rests the unnamed lake that fills the troughs of fresh water that riddle the city.

It was here, in the close-packed stalls of Downmarket, that I got my first real taste of Kaer Maga's storied population. In the centuries since the first squatters stumbled across the vast edifice, Kaer Maga has become a city of outcasts and heretics, a home for those who no longer fit into the societies of their birth. Into this anarchist haven pour the dregs of a score of nations—mostly human, but as different from each other as night and day. Sweettalkers from the far east haggle in their sighs and whistles with hairless Osirion shopkeepers, the lips of the former sewn shut to keep them from uttering anything less than the truename of their god. Veiled men of the Iridian Fold follow close behind their partners, chains and lacquered armor creaking, while farther down a cleric of Abadar ignores the propositions of a Nexian whore-priest. Where so many cultures intersect, tolerance is a virtue, and there are few items or services too taboo to be sold in the claustrophobic markets of Kaer Maga.

It was while I was watching one such transaction that I felt the tug on my belt pouch. Feigning obliviousness, I yawned, then in one movement dropped low and swung my leg around in a heavy arc, sweeping the thief's feet out from under him as I grabbed his arm.

Behind me, a child tumbled to the muddy ground. Dressed in the threadbare rags of a street urchin, he looked perhaps twelve. To my surprise, he grinned up at me shamelessly, hand still firmly in my purse.

"Ha! Good on you, Lord! Got a bit too greedy for my own health now, neh?"

Scrambling nimbly to his feet, the boy gripped the hand that held his wrist and shook it like we had just made a deal.

"Here, now, Sire, I can see how you might be down on my securing of a bit of advance pay without prior notice, but I assure you, I'm worth every copper. The name's Gav, and it's a pleasure to serve. So where to?"

I finally found my voice. "What are you on about?"

"Simple logic, Sire—judging by the way you're eyeing the goods, this is your first time in Kaer Maga,

Gav knows his way around the city, I'll grant him that.

and everyone knows that I'm the best guide these streets have ever seen. So either you can chase me hopelessly through the city I was born in trying to recover this handful of tin in my purse, or you can take me on as your personal guide. Which'll it be?"

His rapid-fire chatter made my head spin, but I couldn't argue the point. Matching the child's professional courtesy, I nodded solemnly and dropped his hand. "I'm looking for a man," I said. "A merchant, I think. Named Dakar."

The boy's demeanor immediately became serious, and he glanced around furtively before pulling me down into a hunker in a narrow alley between stalls.

"You don't start small, do ya, Gov? What do you want to have a run-in with him for?"

"He's got something I need," I said.

"Right, well, see, Dakar isn't someone you just walk in and see. Don't know that any folks have ever seen him. He's what you might call the leader of a merchants' guild up in Ankar-Te." The emphasis he put on "merchant" told me that the man in question was anything but. "You're sure about this?" he asked.

"Yes."

"Alright then." And without another word he stood and moved out into the crowd, darting through cracks between bodies with the ease of a seal in surf, but always staying within sight. After a few moments, he stopped and beckoned. "The Augurs are the straightest shot to the grapevine," he whispered.

"What—" I managed, then stopped short. Before me rose a wall of green flesh covered in bloodstained rags, two piggish eyes staring down at me across a long, thin nose. One hand went to my sword as with the other I sought to push Gav behind me, but the boy was having none of it.

"Greetings, wise Augur," he proclaimed, with a small bow. "This man seeks your insight before an important transaction. Will you part the curtain of days and tell us of what is and may yet be?"

The troll looked me up and down, and I quickly moved my hand away from my sword. Finally it nodded and led us over to a small table near the wall of a smithy. Seating itself across from us, the troll finally spoke, its voice the rumble of a timpani. "What would you ask of tomorrow?" it growled.

Gav held out his hand toward me and snapped his fingers impatiently. I placed a few coins in them, and he deposited several on the table before blatantly pocketing the rest. "This man seeks a business deal with the merchant Dakar, but knows not where to find him. What will result of his search?"

At the mention of the name, the troll's eyes narrowed, and it gave a slight, almost imperceptible nod. Then it stood, drew a knife from a hidden fold in its garment, and before I could move, thrust it into its own belly.

With a sick fascination I watched as the creature pulled the knife across its stomach, spilling its intestines onto the table before us. The child, for his part, watched without blinking as the troll swirled its own bowels with the knifepoint, studying the blood that leaked in hot rivulets across the wood.

"What is sought will be found," the troll intoned at last, "but there will be a price. The blood will flow and will not flow, and the seeker

WHO'S WHO

With so many conflicting cultures and outcasts from conventional society, Kaer Maga can be a confusing place. Presented below are definitions of some of the city's more notable groups, guilds, and organizations.

Ardoc Family: The extensive ruling family of Bis, golem-crafters who wear their chisels as badges of office.

Augurs: Troll soothsayers who use their own innards to prophesize with questionable accuracy.

Bloatmages: Grotesque arcanists who seek power through increased production of blood and lymph.

Brothers of the Seal: An ancient sect of militant monks charged with guarding a magical portal somewhere beneath Kaer Maga. Currently broken into two increasingly violent rival factions: those who wish to open the seal, and those who believe it should remain closed.

Council of Truth: A respected group of scholars devoted to unlocking the secrets of the universe. Disappeared suddenly a generation ago under mysterious conditions, leaving their facilities abandoned.

Duskwardens: A group of urban rangers and warriors devoted to keeping the dark things beneath Kaer Maga from interfering with the city itself. In charge of operating the Halflight Path.

Freemen: An egalitarian gang of escaped slaves that controls the Bottoms.

Sweettalkers: Religious zealots from the far east who, unworthy of speaking their god's true name, choose to sew their own lips shut rather than utter an impure word.

Tallow Boys: The common name for a loose-knit organization of young male prostitutes, many of whom also peddle information collected from their clients.

will be the hand of the handless." Then it scooped up its entrails, thrust them roughly into its gaping belly, and staggered drunkenly away with the coins, one hand holding its already regenerating insides inside.

There was a long pause, and then Gav turned his smug gaze on me again. "There you go, then!" he said.

"What in the Hells was *that?*" I asked, aghast.

"An Augur," he replied. "Troll fortune-tellers. Don't worry, they heal up quick—he'll be fine in a few minutes. And more importantly, Gov, everyone knows they speak the truth—which means they know *everybody*. And he knows we want the word out. We've run up the flag, now we just wait and see who rallies."

He grinned again.

"So, Sire, where are we staying?"

6 Desnus, 4707 AR

Waiting is not my strong suit. A man could explore Kaer Maga for ages and never grow bored, yet returning to the inn each night

THE RING DISTRICTS

The following districts comprise the region of Kaer Maga known as the Ring.

Ankar-Te: This district attracts the most immigrants from the distant south and east. In its narrow streets, child-goddesses locked in ornate metal palanquins mingle with zombie servants and hairless Tallow Boys as they race about doing their masters' bidding.

Bis: Bis's fabled Balconies, a vast swath of residences on the ring's inner walls, are ruled by the golem-crafting Ardoc family, their laws fair but enforced by an army of constructs.

The Bottoms: Escaped slaves and runaways of all sorts are welcomed into the ranks of the Freemen here, their emancipation protected by their well-armed "brothers." They hope someday to grow strong enough to abolish slavery in the other wards.

Cavalcade: Here a number of the streams from the city's unnamed central lake merge before tumbling down the cliff, giving rise to a network of bridges and water-powered workshops.

Highside Stacks: These towers house Kaer Maga's wealthiest citizens, some of whom have never been seen in the city proper, preferring to conduct their business via magic and proxies.

Oriat: Residents of Oriat tend to be cautious and jumpy due to regular outbreaks of guerilla warfare between Brothers of the Seal, which sometimes spill out into public and result in civilian casualties.

Tarheel Promenade: More established than the transient stalls of Downmarket, the bazaars of Tarheel Promenade are particularly known for their concentration of arcane services and temples.

The Warren: This towering shantytown, perched on rickety scaffolding bridging a vast gap in the Ring, houses the city's poorest inhabitants.

having come no closer to my goal is disheartening. At least the kid's impressed—ever since he realized I was a Pathfinder, he's been an endless high-pitched stream of questions about how he can join. I refused to let him in the room the first night, fearing theft, and ever since he's quietly made his exit each night when I retire for the evening. This morning, however, I rose early and found him sleeping in the hallway in front of my door, curled into a ball.

8 Desnus, 4707 AR

My skin reeks of blood.

For several days Gav and I wandered the city, spreading the word of my search through his seemingly limitless stream of contacts and seeing some of the city's more appealing sights: the towers of Highside Stacks that house Kaer Maga's wealthiest residents, and the Balconies in western Bis, where the buildings climb the inner walls of the Ring like cliff-dwellings, a waterfall of humanity that pours out across the stone beneath a ceiling barely visible in the permanent twilight. At first he tried to take

me to the assorted brothels and pleasure-houses of Hospice, but while I was impressed by the variety of delights being offered, some of the more extreme services the painted boys and girls whispered in my ear turned my stomach. Instead we drank in the Bottoms with the escaped slaves that call themselves the Freemen, gambled what we could afford to lose in the exotic gaming halls of Ankar-Te, and saved coin by bathing covertly beneath the bridges of Cavalcade—all accompanied by a running commentary from my surprisingly informed young guide on the city's recent history. The amount of history and petty secrets I amassed in such a short time was astounding, yet everywhere I went, my incomplete task hung over my head like a storm on the horizon, and my purse grew ever lighter.

When contact was made, it was sudden and jarring. While casually browsing a bookseller's stall, I was suddenly yanked backward as my arms were pinioned behind me. Out of a corner of my eye I saw Gav writhing in the clutches of a brawny street tough, and then everything went black as a second pair of hands pulled a bag over my head. I kicked out, catching one of my assailants in the knee with a wet pop, and with the back of my head slammed backward, crushing what felt like a nose. Then something struck me hard in the temple, buckling my legs.

"No more of that, if you want to meet the master," a voice whispered in my ear.

Suspecting I knew who he referred to, I obligingly went limp and felt myself bound and loaded into the back of a cart, which rumbled over cobblestones for some time before finally stopping somewhere far from the bustle of the marketplace. Rough hands pulled me upright and led me through echoing halls of stone or tile before finally stopping and removing my hood, leaving my hands bound.

I was in a stone chamber lit by hanging braziers, the walls draped thickly with silk curtains and tapestries. Along the room's edges sat row upon row of cushions and duvets, accompanied by low wooden tables. At the far end, the room was almost completely obscured by a large paper screen, backlit by a soft yellow light that cast strange shadows. Next to me, two of the thugs removed the bag from a similarly bound Gav before stepping back a respectful distance to watch and listen.

"So," spoke a voice from behind the curtain, "who is this who shouts my name so incautiously about the city?"

I cleared my throat. "My name is Eando Kline, Pathfinder," I replied. "This boy is my guide. I was told by the Magnimarian merchant Belsir Trullos that the man known as Dakar could provide me with something I seek—a gem of some importance to my society; it's known as an ioun stone. I come prepared to bargain."

"And what do you have to offer?" the voice asked.

"My organization is ill-disposed toward secrets," I responded, attempting to regain control of the situation and put us on equal footing. "Why not dispense with the cheap theatrics? I like to know what sort of man I'm dealing with."

The guards stiffened, but the voice gave a soft, hissing laugh. With a rustle and the sound of something heavy being dragged, Dakar emerged from behind the curtain.

He was huge. His face was long and narrow, with a prominent chin and hooked nose, the hairless skin stretched tight over his skull. Sweeping back from his bald forehead, an elaborate headdress of overlapping, bejewled plates clinked and rattled. Beneath that, however, any resemblance to humanity ceased. From the neck down, his body was that of an enormous serpent, dark gray and wrapped in places with ornate golden bangles. He slithered to a stop in front of us and laughed again at our expressions, forked tongue flickering between his teeth.

"Wormfolk!" Gav breathed.

"We prefer the term 'naga,' child," Dakar admonished. "It would serve you well to remember that. Now, Kline, I have freely granted your request, though to do so is not often in my nature. What do you have to offer me?"

"Gold," I replied, finding my voice once again. "Gold and information. Access to the knowledge of the Pathfinders, as vetted by myself."

The naga made a nest of his coils and reclined upon them, eyes locked unsettlingly on my own.

"Do you really think I need either, Eando Kline?" he asked. "I have eyes and ears in every corner of Kaer Maga—if I wish to know something, I know it. And your wealth is but a drop in the sea as compared to mine. No, Pathfinder, I deal in neither, but rather in service and favors. And I have one prepared for you."

I stood silent, neither accepting nor rejecting anything.

He nodded. "Good. As you have no doubt gleaned from your adolescent companion, I operate a number of enterprises in this district, and help maintain peace in the city through strategic arrangements with professionals in similar trades. Recently, however, an upstart has been attempting to circumvent these gentlemen's agreements and move in on my territory. Neshiel is a hemotheurge—a bloatmage, as some might call them." He glanced pointedly at Gav, who blushed but stood tall under the gaze. "The wizard recently had the audacity to steal a valuable spellbook from one of the hex crafters under my protection, and I want you to get it back... and deliver a message in the process."

"Why can't you send one of your men?" I asked.

The snake-man tossed his head in what I interpreted as a shrug. "It's complicated," he replied, his forked tongue darting out to taste the air. "A matter of guild agreements and powerful persons who must be appeased. Suffice to say that the known free agents can't be trusted and I'm not interested in risking my own boys. Still, it should be a simple enough matter, if you have the stomach for it. I'll even let you borrow something to make the task a little easier."

From behind the curtain, a tiny object floated up and over to me as if of its own accord: an amulet on a worn leather thong, carved from black volcanic glass into the coiled shape of a leech.

"While you wear that amulet, the magic of the bloatmage will be unable to touch you," Dakar said.

I stared at it uncertainly. "I'm no assassin," I said.

"Certainly not," Dakar soothed. "But unless I miss my guess, you know how to handle yourself in a fight. And besides, Neshiel's impertinence endangers the exceedingly fragile web of alliances that keeps this city from tearing itself apart. By putting some fear into him, you'll save countless lives. Think on that." There was an expectant pause.

"Alright," I said at last, slipping the amulet over my head. "When do you need this task completed?"

The naga smiled.

"No time like the present," he said.

Thus I found myself, only a few hours later, standing outside a prosperous shop in Tarheel Promenade, while Gav peered into the

Dakar isn't quite the man I had expected.

BLOATMAGES

Hemotheurges, more commonly known as bloatmages, are spellcasters who use blood as a key component in their magic. As common lore holds that sorcerous ability is inherited naturally through bloodlines, bloatmages overload their own circulatory systems, producing more blood than they require in order to amplify their natural ability, frequently using the excess as a component in arcane rituals. As a result, bloatmages' skins distend grossly as vessels burst and blood pools in rolls of bruised, engorged fat.

With their bodies so delicately balanced at their bursting point, bloatmages must be careful to regularly let their own blood in precise amounts, usually through the strategic placement of dozens of leeches. Without such measures, the increased pressure on a bloatmage's brain causes him to lose most of his higher cognitive functions and fly into an insane rage, lashing out both physically and magically. If the hemorrhaging bloatmage is not immediately bled in this situation, organs buckle under the strain and he quickly lapses into seizures and dies.

Although evil bloatmages have been known to collect the blood of others or form symbiotic relationships with vampires, most bloatmages are scholarly ascetics concerned primarily with unlocking greater power through the blending of sorcery and wizardry than either is capable of alone.

him there. His hands darted in quick gestures as he mumbled half-heard words, a glow of blue fire springing from his fingers and forming a net around me, only to evaporate the second it touched my skin. Against my chest, the amulet glowed red with warmth. He saw it, and his eyes widened with fear.

"What do you want?" he asked.

"Dakar sends his regards," I replied. "Where's the book?"

He launched into a stream of curses, cut off only when my hand constricted his windpipe. I looked up from where I crouched over his bulk on the floor and saw Gav watching the exchange with open-mouthed excitement.

"Wait outside and keep a lookout," I told him.

"But—" he began.

"Gav, *outside.*"

He stomped out of the room and I looked down at Neshiel, his face twisted with anger and fear. "Well?" I asked.

He glared and clenched his jaw. Inspecting the bulbous flesh, I selected a particularly large leech and pulled, ripping it from his skin and dropping it wriggling to the floor.

He gasped at the pain, but only a few drops of blood welled from the puckered wound where the parasite had attached itself. I gave him a pointed look.

He spat, hitting me on the chin. I reached down and pulled another leech. And another.

He glared and clenched his jaw. Inspecting the bulbous flesh, I selected a particularly large leech and pulled, ripping it from his skin and dropping it wriggling to the floor.

half-light for anyone who looked suspicious. He gave the all-clear, and together we moved into the building.

The shop itself was a vast collection of magical oddities: disembodied hands and floating orbs that flickered through every color of the spectrum. Gav's eyes immediately lit up with greed, but I shook my head slightly and he caught the motion. We were here on a mission—we were not thieves.

Sitting behind the shop's counter, Neshiel was exactly how Dakar had described him. Obviously once human, his skin was now expanded outward as if inflated, the rolls of bloated flesh crisscrossed everywhere with varicose veins. Beneath the surface, fluid oozed and eddied, his skin one vast blister. And across this gluttonous expanse stretched dozens of fat black leeches. He looked up and smiled as we walked in, revealing a set of perfect white teeth that somehow made the whole package that much more horrible.

"Welcome, Lords!" he called in a deep, jovial voice. "What wonders of the arcane can Neshiel provide?"

I wasted no time. Without saying a word, I strode quickly across the room. Neshiel's smile flickered and faltered, and then my outstretched hand met his doughy neck and knocked him completely off his stool, slamming him to the floor and pinning

As I plucked the things from the hemotheurge's skin, a curious change began to take place. None of the wounds bled more than a few drops, and indeed they seemed to heal remarkably quickly, but by the time half of the leeches lay crushed in a pile by my feet, his face was flushed and his breathing labored. Beneath me his flesh seemed to expand and grow taught, the vessels in his eyes distending until the whites were solid red. I ripped off two more leeches, and trickles of blood began to flow from his nose and ears. Beneath me his skin was swollen and purple, a balloon ready to pop. Finally he screamed, and I ceased my stomach-churning ministrations.

"There!" he gasped, pointing to a drawer in the counter. "Book... there... take...." He seemed to be having trouble finding the words, and with a shock I suddenly wondered if the swelling in his flesh had extended to his brain. Standing and yanking open the drawer, I found a thick leather book with gold piping that matched Dakar's specifications. I picked it up and walked around the counter. Behind me, Neshiel moaned and pressed wounded leeches to his face, sobbing with relief.

As I neared the exit, I caught a glimpse of movement through a cracked door that I'd walked heedlessly past in the excitement. Flinging it open with my hand on my sword, I found myself confronted with a child. Eyes wide, the toddler couldn't have been more than

THE CORE DISTRICTS

The central part of Kaer Maga consists of these three districts.

Downmarket: Common lore holds that you can find anything you want in this crowded market of wagons and stalls, no matter how rare or taboo—as long as you can pay the often steep prices.

Hospice: Catering to visitors and residents alike, the inns and bordellos of Hospice specialize in a wide variety of cultural comforts and fetishes, earning a reputation as the most lavish (and morally decrepit) red light district in Varisia.

Widdershins: Merchants and middle-class citizens without ties to any of the ruling factions tend to settle in this relatively peaceful residential neighborhood, maintaining a well-paid constabulary to keep it that way.

two or three. On his flesh, corpulent with baby fat, sat two small leeches. He looked up at me in concern, then back to the sniveling mass of Neshiel. Both bore the same sparse brown mop of hair.

I pushed past him and out the door. Gav greeted me with enthusiasm. "What happened?" he asked, trying to look around me into the shop. "Did you get it?"

I felt sick.

"Let's go," I said.

Back at the Sorry Excuse, I sat at a splintered table and twirled Dakar's gem lightly over my fingers, making it appear and disappear. Even while dormant, the stone still sent faint vibrations down my arm, as if the limb were reawakening after falling asleep. Three empty pints and a hyperactive Gav kept me company, the latter still high from our second exchange with a real-life crime boss.

"...and that's how I would have taken him if you got in trouble," he finished, finally pausing for breath. "So where to next?"

I stopped flipping the tiny green crystal and replaced it inside my shirt, where it rested by my wayfinder in a pouch next to my chest.

"Well, out of this accursed city, for starters," I replied. "Hopefully before this whole thing comes back to bite me. Then find someone headed back to Korvosa and post some letters, maybe even stop in there myself."

"Sounds great," he said, flashing me that winning smile. "When do we leave?"

I stopped short and looked down into his open, trusting face. This kid had nothing to tie him here, I realized. No family, no support network, just the living he scratched out on the streets through his wits. Not that different from me, really. And now here I was, a chance for him to be a part of something larger, to transcend the day-to-day. I knew the feeling all too well, and confronted with those hopeful eyes, I couldn't tell him no.

"Alright," I said at last, taking some coins from my pouch and scratching a quick list on a slip of paper. "First order of business, as junior member of this expedition, you go pick up these supplies while I stay here and have another drink. You got it handled?" I raised my hand to order another mug from the barkeep.

"No problem, sir! Back in a blink!" And then he was out the door, sprinting with heedless abandon through the mass of shoppers.

I sat there for a full minute, watching the crowd beyond the doors. Then I stood and hoisted my bag, the drink untouched. Walking out the door, I looked one last time in the direction Gav had gone, then turned and strode quickly the other way.

The kid was sharp, there was no doubt about that. He'd make a good Pathfinder someday.

But I work alone.

Only constant leeching keeps bloatmages from hemorrhaging.

BESTIARY

SIZE COMPARISON

```
35
30
25
20
15
10
 6
 5
 4
 3
 2
 1
 0
```

Hook Mountain is no place to go wandering alone. In addition to ogres, giants, and all manner of wild and hungry beasts, other terrors—creatures as crooked and brutal as the peak upon which they make their home—scour the stony mountain heights.

This month, the Bestiary presents six rugged and ravenous denizens of Hook Mountain, along with a number of other beasts known to haunt the fringes of civilization—all from the overactive pen of Nick Logue. Both the ogrekin and the Mother of Oblivion Black Magga feature prominently in "The Hook Mountain Massacre." The other beasts—the argorth, totenmaske, skull ripper, and smoke

haunt—might also find places haunting the environs around Hook Mountains or in future adventures of your own.

GMs looking to involve these beasts in their Rise of the Runelords campaign might add vague rumors of an argorth that sleeps in the hills near Fort Rannick, possibly foreshadowing future threats for the new owners of the keep. Secluded communities like Turtleback Ferry also make appealing hunting grounds for shapechangers like totenmaskes and smoke haunts seeking wandering huntsmen to prey upon. And who knows what lurks in the deepest tunnels of Skull's Crossing? A skullripper might still guard the ancient dam for its forgotten masters.

SMOKE HAUNT

The smell of wood smoke bears the taint of burning flesh. A branch in the campfire sputters and hisses. From within the fire's embers a smoldering skull glares out, its eyes wells of cold darkness. Tendrils of smoke dance around and through it like tongues or writhing snakes.

SMOKE HAUNT   CR 4

Always CE Small undead (fire)

Init +9; **Senses** darkvision 60 ft.; Listen +2, Spot +2

Aura lifedrinking (20 ft.), smoke patterns (20 ft.)

DEFENSE

AC 20, touch 20, flat-footed 15

   (+5 Dexterity, +4 natural, +1 size)

hp 39 (6d12)

Fort +2, **Ref** +9, **Will** +7

Defensive Abilities undead traits; **Immune** fire

Weaknesses vulnerable to cold

OFFENSE

Spd fly 50 ft. (perfect)

Melee slam +9 (1d3 plus 2d6 negative energy)

Spell-Like Abilities (CL 5th, +9 ranged)

   3/day—*ghost sound* (DC 14), *heat metal* (DC 16), *scorching ray*

   1/day—*deep slumber* (DC 17), *fire shield*, *suggestion* (DC 17)

TACTICS

Before Combat A smoke haunt uses its flameseer ability to find prospective prey, then teleports nearby.

During Combat A smoke haunt hides in flames, letting its lifedrinking ability weaken those nearby.

Morale A smoke haunt flees if detected.

STATISTICS

Str —, **Dex** 20, **Con** —, **Int** 8, **Wis** 15, **Cha** 19

Base Atk +3; **Grp** —

Feats Dodge, Improved Initiative, Lightning Reflexes

Skills Hide +18, Move Silently +14, Tumble +14

Languages Common

SQ flameseer, flamewalker

ECOLOGY

Environment cold forests and mountains

Organization solitary

Treasure none

Advancement 7–18 HD (Small)

Level Adjustment —

SPECIAL ABILITIES

Flameseer (Su) A smoke haunt can sense any fire of torch size or larger within a half mile. By concentrating, it can peer through such flames as if using *clairaudience/clairvoyance*.

Flamewalker (Su) Once per day, a smoke haunt can use *greater teleport* to appear in any fire of Small size or larger. When a smoke haunt teleports into a fire, it can make a Hide check as part of the teleportation to avoid notice from any creatures nearby.

Lifedrinking (Su) A smoke haunt feeds on the heat of the living. A haunt seems to shed soothing warmth, but this is actually the sensation of life

being absorbed by the ravenous undead. Any living creature within 20 feet of a smoke haunt must make a DC 17 Fortitude save or take 2d6 points of negative energy damage. A victim who fails to resist this attack feels warm and complacent, having no idea he has taken any damage unless he makes a DC 15 Wisdom check. If a victim makes this save, he feels strangely weak, but does not necessarily notice the smoke haunt. The save DCs are Charisma-based.

Smoke Patterns (Su) A smoke haunt exudes coils of smoke whenever it is surrounded by a fire of Small size or larger. Anyone within 20 feet of a smoke haunt immersed in fire must make a DC 17 Will save or become entranced by the eerie patterns formed amid the rising smoke, taking a –4 penalty on Listen and Spot checks and a –2 penalty on Will saves for as long as the smoke haunt remains in range. This is a mind-affecting pattern. A creature that successfully saves against this ability cannot be affected by the same smoke haunt's smoke patterns for 24 hours. The save DC is Charisma-based.

Said to form from the spirits of lost wanderers slain by exposure and despair, smoke haunts hunger for life, warmth, and a home they're cursed to never find again.

Ecology

Appearing as little more than a skull wreathed in fire nestled deep in the embers of a campfire or hearth, these evil spirits are only content when bathed in flame and with living souls nearby to feed off.

Habitat & Society

Smoke haunts hate all things, even others of their own kind. They hunt alone. These undead menaces dwell in remote reaches with long nights and short days, misty moors, or rugged mountains where travelers and explorers provide them the nourishment they require.

TOTENMASKE

An emaciated, almost skeletal humanoid thing ambles forward. The movement of its bones is clearly visible beneath its moldy green skin, its ribs pushing taut against thin flesh as if they might burst free at any second. The thing's long spindly arms end in bony protrusions more than a foot long, which scrape against the ground as it comes. Upon its malformed blister of a head gapes an oversized mouth, which looks more like a yawning, infected wound set with broken, pointed teeth.

TOTENMASKE   CR 7

Always NE Medium undead

Init +12; **Senses** darkvision 60 ft.; Listen +17, Spot +17

DEFENSE

AC 23, touch 18, flat-footed 15

    (+8 Dexterity, +5 natural)

hp 78 (12d12)

Fort +4, **Ref** +14, **Will** +10

Defensive Abilities undead traits; **Resist** cold 20

OFFENSE

Spd 50 ft., burrow 10 ft.

Melee 2 claws +14 (1d6+3) and

    bite +9 (2d8+1 plus devour memories)

Special Attacks death mask, devour memories, fleshdrinking, shape flesh

TACTICS

Before Combat A totenmaske prefers that its prey not realize the

    danger it presents, either hiding and stalking its quarry or approaching

    directly in the guise of a past victim.

During Combat If its disguise is penetrated, a totenmaske first

    attempts to eat the memories of those who realize its true

    nature. If this fails, it goes to grisly work with its claws and drinks

    deep of its opponent's flesh and dreams.

Morale Totenmaskes are cowards by nature and only fight to drink flesh so

    as to once again experience a shadow of life and revel in desire and sin.

    If reduced to fewer than half its hit points, a totenmaske flees.

STATISTICS

Str 16, **Dex** 26, **Con** 10, **Int** 16, **Wis** 14, **Cha** 20

Base Atk +6; **Grp** +9

Feats Combat Expertise, Combat Reflexes, Improved Initiative,

    Lightning Reflexes, Weapon Finesse

Skills Disguise +20, Hide +23, Jump +28, Listen +17, Move Silently

    +23, Spot +17, Tumble +25

Languages Abyssal, Celestial, Common, Infernal

ECOLOGY

Environment any

Organization solitary

Treasure standard

Advancement 13–16 HD (Medium), 17–24 HD (Large)

Level Adjustment —

SPECIAL ABILITIES

Death Mask (Su) As a standard action, a totenmaske can take

    the shape and appearance of the last creature against which it

    used its fleshdrinking power. The totenmaske can shake off the

    disguised flesh as a free action, but then cannot resume the form

until it drinks flesh from that creature again. The totenmaske's disguise is temporary and grows more and more unstable as days pass. At first, a totenmaske gains a +10 on Disguise checks to impersonate the subject, but every day this bonus is reduced by 2 as its flesh begins to droop and strange inconsistencies develop (one eye might bulge, the right side of its mouth might droop, or a sliver of bone could protrude from the side of its hand). Unless the totenmaske drinks the flesh of the subject again, its mask rots off entirely when the Disguise bonus granted by this ability reaches +0 after 5 days.

Devour Memories (Su) A totenmaske can eat the memories and dreams of a creature it bites. The target must make a DC 21 Will save or have his thoughts drained, taking 1d4 points of Charisma drain. A totenmaske gains a +4 bonus on Disguise checks made to impersonate a victim whose memories it has drained at any point in the past. The save DC is Charisma-based.

Fleshdrinking (Su) If a creature is hit by both of a totenmaske's claw attacks, his flesh is partially drained away by the totenmaske's hollow claws. This attack deals 1d4 points of Constitution damage and leaves the victim sickened for 1d4 rounds. On each use of this ability, a totenmaske gains 5 temporary hit points.

Shape Flesh (Su) By spending a minute in contact with a helpless creature, a totenmaske can reshape its victim's face, causing flesh to cover vital features. The target must make a DC 21 Fortitude save or have his face physically altered. A totenmaske can use this ability on one of four different features per use.

    Ears: Flesh covers the victim's ears, leaving him deaf.

    Eyes: Flesh covers the victim's eyes, rendering him permanently blind.

    Mouth: Flesh covers the victim's mouth, preventing him from speaking or eating.

    Nose: Flesh covers the victim's nose, preventing the use of the scent ability and making him immune to scent-based attacks.

    This ability functions only on living creatures whose bodies are composed mostly of flesh. A totenmaske can use this ability multiple times on the same creature. Reshaping multiple features can lead to more deadly results, such as suffocation if the nose and mouth are covered (see page 304 of the DMG).

    The effects of this ability are permanent, but can be reversed with a *heal* or *restoration* spell. Alternatively, someone can surgically reopen the sealed features with a successful DC 25 Heal check. The attempt deals 1d6 points of damage whether or not it is successful. The save DC is Charisma-based.

Accursed by fell powers, the souls of some sinners do not rest easy. They lie cold in shallow unmarked graves, or litter sites of slaughter forgotten by the living. From these sin-blasted carcasses horrors called totenmaskes arise. Doomed to feel nothing but agony, hunger, and desire, these creatures endlessly seek to satisfy the sinful appetites they possessed in life, drinking the flesh of living creatures, eating dreams and memories, robbing flesh, and stepping into their victim's very lives to enjoy a lover's caress or feel the touch of wind and sunlight on their stolen skin.

A totenmaske can be created from the corpse of an appropriately sinful evil mortal by a cleric of 18th level or higher with the *create greater undead* spell.

Ecology

Sinister and cunning, a totenmaske lives only to prey on the living. It does not drink blood or sap another's soul, but rather craves only sin. Passionate sexual release, the taste of cooked meat, the feel of silk finery, cool water, or even pain—all are earthly delights beyond its lifeless carcass. A totenmaske is not interested in killing foes as much as it wants to become them completely and revel in the desires of the flesh once more. It seeks out targets it will enjoy replacing—usually a comely or wealthy creature capable of sating its deathless desires. The foul undead then drinks deep of its target's flesh, and if possible imprisons its victim alive so as to continue impersonating him as long as it wishes. Its curse is rot and decay. No stolen flesh remains uncorrupted for long upon a totenmaske's unnatural reeking corpse, and so it hunts always for more victims and even greater pleasures.

Habitat & Society

Totenmaskes lair near or in populated areas. They favor out-of-the-way and overlooked regions of otherwise bustling cities, where they might hide away living victims in crumbling tenements, mournful graveyards, or abandoned lighthouses while they live out their stolen lives. Totenmaskes crave contact and community wherein they can pursue their sins, but their jealous natures ensure they rarely work in concert with others of their kind, as they do not share their pleasures easily.

Some particularly sin-starved totenmaskes track their obscene heritages all the way back to ancient Thassilon, endlessly seeking ways to escape their tomb-prisons and again prey upon the living.

Treasure

Totenmaskes are as greedy as they are lustful and violent, and they collect hoards of wealth to satisfy their avaricious urges. They favor gaudy jewels and other items of extravagance, whose sparkle and luster temporarily soothe their burning desires like balm on an angry insect sting.

Variants

In the gold and lapis lazuli vault-crypts of the near-mythic lost city of Ird, hundreds of brash explorers and trap-slain pillagers have become the hidden metropolis's most deadly guardians. These totenmaskes have become infused with the gold and gemstones they once coveted.

Burial Mask (Su) The totenmaske takes the form of the last creature it used its fleshdrinking ability upon, appearing as a gold and gem-studded statue of its victim. The totenmaske is obviously not the creature imitated and gains no bonus to its Disguise check. Instead it gains a +5 bonus to its natural Armor Class for as long as it retains this form. In addition, any creature that sees the totenmaske must make a DC 21 Will save or be fascinated for as long as the totenmaske is in sight. The creature whose appearance the totenmaske is currently duplicating takes a –4 penalty on this Will save. If a totenmaske attacks a creature fascinated by it, the fascination immediately ends and the creature cannot be fascinated with that totenmaske again for 24 hours. The appearance of this statue gradually melts and distorts over the course of five days, after which the creature loses its AC bonus and reverts to normal. The save DC is Charisma-based.

SKULL RIPPER

A fearsome chittering heralds the approach of this morbid monstrosity. A giant headless scorpion-like thing of blackened bone and chitin rounds the corner ahead, scuttling along the wall as its two pincers snap ominously. A long grisly tail composed of dozens of chattering skulls arches up over its back. Some of the skulls are ancient and bleached white, while others are recent trophies still shrouded in rotting cheeks, their jellied eyes rolling madly in their sockets. A curved bony tip protrudes from the last skull of its tail, its deadly point smeared with poison.

SKULL RIPPER — CR 9

Usually CN Large construct

Init +3; **Senses** darkvision 60 ft.; Listen +1, Spot +1

Aura dread visage (30 feet)

DEFENSE

AC 24, touch 12, flat-footed 21

    (+4 armor, +3 Dexterity, +8 natural, –I size)

hp 112 (15d10+30)

Fort +5, **Ref** +10, **Will** +6

DR 5/adamantine; **Immune** construct traits; **Resist** cold 10; **SR** 20

OFFENSE

Spd 40 ft., climb 40 ft.

Melee 2 claws +19 (2d6+9/19–20) and

    sting +13 (1d10+4 plus poison)

Space 10 ft.; **Reach** 10 ft.

Special Attacks behead, improved grab

TACTICS

Before Combat A skull ripper watches its prey from afar. The creature then sets a deadly ambush, waiting for foes to draw within range of its gibbering skulls before setting the gristly trophies rattling.

During Combat A skull ripper fixates on the heads of its enemies, attempting to slow them with its poison and then behead those unable to escape.

Morale Most skull rippers retreat from combat when reduced below 15 hit points.

STATISTICS

Str 28, **Dex** 16, **Con** —, **Int** 5, **Wis** 13, **Cha** 12

Base Atk +11; **Grp** +24

Feats Combat Reflexes, Lightning Reflexes, Improved Critical (claw), Power Attack, Stealthy, Weapon Focus (claw)

Skills Hide +10, Move Silently +14

Languages Thassilonian (cannot speak)

ECOLOGY

Environment any

Organization solitary

Treasure standard

Advancement 16–23 HD (Large), 24–31 HD (Huge)

Level Adjustment —

SPECIAL ABILITIES

Behead (Ex) The skull ripper is an expert at collecting its favorite trophies—skulls—and once it's grappled a foe, it can try to behead its victim with a single gut-wrenching rip. This attempt to tear off the victim's head deals 4d6+18 points of damage—if this damage is enough to bring the foe to fewer than 0 hit points, the victim is beheaded and instantly slain.

Dread Visage (Su) Skull rippers are particularly fearsome in appearance, and any creature that is within 30 feet and can see the skull ripper must make a DC 18 Will save each round to avoid becoming frightened. If any of the heads affixed to the skull ripper are recognizable associates of a particular character, that character takes a –4 penalty on this saving throw. A character that makes the save is immune to the dread visage of that particular skull ripper for 24 hours. This is a mind-affecting fear effect. The save DC is Charisma-based.

Improved Grab (Su) To use this ability, a skull ripper must hit a creature of its size or smaller with both claw attacks. It can then attempt to start a grapple as a free action without provoking an attack of opportunity. If it wins the grapple check, it establishes a hold and can attempt to behead the target.

Poison (Ex) Injury, Fortitude DC 17, initial and secondary damage 2d4 Dex. The save DC is Constitution-based.

A skull ripper is a plague on the living. There is nothing that gives it more satisfaction than wrenching a man's head from his neck, then holding it aloft to show the victim's bulging, still-seeing eyes his own decapitated corpse thrashing and twitching in a gory puddle of its own juices. The skull ripper then slides the head onto its long, grim tail in a grotesque display, the head's screams dying away as it joins the beast's repulsive collection. The skull ripper lives for the hunt, and its dark existence is driven only by a desire to collect further trophies from the dead.

History

The constructs known today as skull rippers were once guardians of the dead, the grim custodians of the great ossuaries of Thassilon. When a particularly wealthy Thassilonian noble died, the members of his household would commission a great tomb into which the deceased lord would be placed along with extensive treasures, large numbers of slaves—and one skull ripper. There, in the utter darkness of a sealed tomb, the still air would resound with screams as the slaves were harvested, one by one, in a final grisly pageant for the dead lord's entertainment. As each head was removed, the chittering construct would affix the trophy to its chitinous carapace.

After the collapse of the Thassilonian Empire, such rites became much less common as wide swaths of the lower castes rebelled against such wanton abuses of power, and over time the skull rippers were forgotten. Yet many of these grisly constructs still wait in silence behind forgotten doors and buried beneath the dirt of ages, watching for those who would dare to disturb their lords.

Habitat & Society

Although most skull rippers are discovered in ancient tombs and sepulchers, occasionally geological upheaval or flooding destroys a given catacomb or leaves a skull ripper stranded. In these cases, the constructs emerge and venture forth into the world above, harvesting skulls and causing widespread panic as it searches for a similar tomb in which to take up residence. Should two skull rippers encounter each other, they fight savagely in an attempt to harvest each other's skulls, resulting in the destruction of at least one of the constructs.

Treasure

On occasion, a skull ripper becomes so obsessed with its collection of skulls that it adorns them with rich, lustrous jewels and plates of precious metal. The older skulls on a skull ripper's tail sometimes have high-quality rubies, emeralds, sapphires, or similar gems lodged in their eye sockets (3d6×100 gp total worth).

As most skull rippers trace their creation to an era forgotten thousands of years ago, even the most mundane items fused into their morbid carapaces might be invaluable historical artifacts. Simplest remnants—like pottery, bits of armor, brass tools, and the like—might have a value several thousand gold pieces higher than their modern equivalents. Finding a buyer capable of recognizing such artifacts' worth (with a DC 20 Appraise or Knowledge [history] check) might require a trip to an arcane college, museum, or other similar community of scholars.

Construction

A skull ripper is a construct made entirely from the carcasses of dead things. The basic shape of its body, with its powerful serrated claws and wickedly barbed tail, comes from the exoskeleton of an ember scorpion, a species of Large monstrous scorpion native to Varisia. Onto this frame is grafted the ribcage of a giant, as well as innumerable smaller bones from other creatures, which reinforce the frame and give the construct much of its fearsome appearance. Lastly, thousands of tiny shards and spurs of bone are driven into every available surface. Once animated, the construct is capable of flexing these spurs to latch onto any skulls placed on its carapace, as well as improving its ability to grab and hold its prey. All of these material components can be harvested by the caster or purchased from shady adventurers for roughly 500 gp in total (incorporated into the final cost).

Assembling the body requires a DC 15 Knowledge (architecture and engineering) or a DC 15 Heal check.

CL 10th; Craft Construct (see MM 303), *animate dead, fear, geas/quest, keen edge, limited wish*, caster must be at least 10th level; Price 30,000 gp; Cost 15,500 gp + 1,200 XP.

Controlling a Skull Ripper

Skull rippers were created to be the grim servants of Thassilonian nobles, and as such have an innate desire to obey their masters. While they obey their masters implicitly, if a character can demonstrate magical power by casting an arcane spell where the skull ripper can notice it, and then making a DC 35 Spellcraft check, the caster may then give the construct commands for a period of 24 hours, provided those commands are spoken aloud in Thassilonian. After 24 hours, the skull ripper's memory becomes fuzzy and it becomes obstinate and slow to respond, requiring another display of arcane power if a character besides its master tries to command it.

Skull Rippers in Varisia

While skull rippers and their construction have been almost completely forgotten in modern Varisia, the havoc one causes when it wanders into a populated area is guaranteed to inspire tales and legends. Most of the skull rippers encountered in recent years are the result of the blue dragon Cadrilkasta's excavation of the great Thassilonian sepulcher known as Guiltspur. As each new level of silent tombs is breached and exposed to light, the resident skull rippers emerge to do battle, slaughtering all in their path. To the great dragon, these are mere nuisances that cost her valuable digging slaves, and she fights them only long enough to drive them away from her work in search of other victims.

ARGORTH

An avalanche of gnashing teeth, bone hooks, and worm coils roils forward in a wave of sundering parts. At the forefront of this thrashing, tentacular body yawns a howling pit of a mouth, ringed with a spiral of churning teeth and three massive, spiked mandibles.

ARGORTH   CR 11

Always CE Huge aberration

Init +3; **Senses** blindsight 120 ft.; Listen +3, Spot +3

DEFENSE

AC 26, touch 11, flat-footed 23

(+3 Dexterity, +15 natural, –2 size)

hp 138 (12d8+84); Diehard

Fort +15, **Ref** +7, **Will** +11

DR 10/cold iron; **Immune** gaze attacks, mind-affecting effects, visual effects; **Resist** acid 10, cold 20; **SR** 21

OFFENSE

Spd 40 ft., burrow 20 ft., climb 20 ft., swim 40 ft.

Melee bite +19 (3d6+11) and

tail slam +13 (2d6+5)

Space 15 ft.; **Reach** 10 ft.

Special Attacks constrict 2d6+16, fearful shriek, ground slam, improved grab, swallow whole

TACTICS

Before Combat Maddened engines of destruction, argorths use their fearful shriek ability and then rampage into battle.

During Combat Once engaged, argorths attempt to swallow as many creatures as they can, using their ground slam ability to devastate wide areas.

Morale Argorths know no fear and fight until destroyed.

STATISTICS

Str 32, **Dex** 16, **Con** 24, **Int** 8, **Wis** 16, **Cha** 20

Base Atk +9; **Grp** +28

Feats Cleave, Combat Reflexes, Die Hard, Endurance, Weapon Focus (bite)

Skills Climb +19, Spot +18, Swim +19

Languages Abyssal

SQ death throes

ECOLOGY

Environment temperate or cold mountains

Organization solitary

Treasure standard

Advancement 13–24 HD (Huge), 25–36 HD (Gargantuan)

Level Adjustment —

SPECIAL ABILITIES

Blindsight (Ex) An argorth can ascertain the location of all creatures within 120 feet. Beyond that range it is considered blinded. Argorths are invulnerable to gaze attacks, visual effects of spells such as illusions, and other attack forms that rely on sight.

Constrict (Ex) An argorth deals 2d6+16 points of damage with a successful grapple check.

Death Throes (Ex) When an argorth is reduced to –10 hit points, it collapses to the ground and thrashes wildly. It gets one final tail slam

attack on every creature within 10 feet, after which it dies. It cannot grapple or constrict with this final attack.

Fearful Shriek (Su) An argorth can emit a wholly unnatural shriek, a howl not of the mortal world. When an argorth uses this ability, all creatures within 100 feet must succeed on a DC 21 Will save or be shaken for as long as the monster remains in sight. This is a sonic mind-affecting fear effect. This ability does not affect creatures with more Hit Dice than the argorth. Whether or not the save is successful, an affected creature is immune to the same argorth's fearful shriek for 24 hours. The save DC is Charisma-based.

Ground Slam (Ex) As a full-round action, an argorth can lift its entire body into the air and slam it against the ground in a single, reckless attack. This attack deals 1d10 points of damage to the argorth, but all creatures within 5 feet of the monster are targeted by this +13 melee attack which deals 2d8+16 points of damage. Any creature standing within 10 feet of an argorth when it makes this attack (including those who might be damaged) must make a DC 23 Reflex save or be knocked prone by the sheer force of the blow. The save DC is Constitution-based.

Improved Grab (Su) To use this ability, an argorth must hit a creature at least one size category smaller than itself with its tail. It can then attempt to start a grapple as a free action without provoking an attack of opportunity. If it wins the grapple check, it establishes a hold and can constrict.

Swallow Whole (Ex) An argorth can try to swallow a grabbed Medium or smaller opponent by making a successful grapple check. An argorth that swallows an opponent can use its Cleave feat to bite and grab another opponent.

A swallowed creature takes 2d8+8 points of bludgeoning damage and 8 points of acid damage per round from the argorth's gizzard. A swallowed creature can cut its way out by using a light slashing or piercing weapon to deal 25 points of damage to the gizzard (AC 15). Once the creature exits, muscular action closes the hole; another swallowed opponent must cut its own way out.

An argorth's gizzard can hold 2 Medium, 8 Small, 32 Tiny, or 128 Diminutive or smaller opponents.

Skills: An argorth has a +8 racial bonus on Climb checks and can always choose to take 10 on a Climb check, even if rushed or threatened. It also has a +8 racial bonus on any Swim check to perform some special action or avoid a hazard. It can always choose to take 10 on a Swim check, even if distracted or endangered. It can use the run action while swimming, provided it swims in a straight line.

The horrifying, incomprehensible spawn of the Mothers of Oblivion, these titans of destruction are weaned on bloodshed and the dark dreams of Lamashtu herself. Nearly 30 feet tall, these marauding tentacles know only rage and slaughter, laying waste to whole regions, paving the way for their dark mistresses' hordes of ravening monsters. Unnatural disasters, argorths have more in common with hurricanes and volcanos than the beasts of the natural world.

Ecology

Argorths are tentacles split from the unreasoning anatomy of a Mother of Oblivion. Shed by the massive servants of Lamashtu after acts of incredible bloodshed and malice, argorths grow to full size in a matter of minutes and skitter away to wreak massacres of their own. Dozens of rubbery black appendages unsheathe from their sinewy, worm-like bodies, and all are studded with bony saws and flesh-hungry hooks. Argorths have no apparent face or eyes, but great maws riddled with jutting teeth-blades sprout from their massive serpentine forms. Lacking sight, argorths detect the world around them through a combination of heightened bloodsense and taste facilitated by thousands of coarse black hairs covering their body, lending them their blindsight. Unnatural beings twice over, argorths have no role in any sane ecology, existing only to indulge in ever-greater orgies of destruction. Argorths require no food and no rest.

Habitat & Society

Argorths wander seemingly without aim, leaving vast swaths of devastation in their wake. Seeking slaughter and destruction, they actively avoid lands despoiled by others of their kind, yet, as they are so extraordinarily rare, this is rarely a problem. While the Mother of Monsters delights in letting her grandchildren roam, occasionally she implants a direction into an argorth's fury-clouded mind, sending it as an executor of her wrath or harbinger of her armies. She has also been known to put argorths into deep, centuries-long torpors, hiding them away and preserving the beasts for unknown future plots.

Treasure

Argorths have no interest in treasure. The possessions of their victims are left as broken shards in the wake of their cataclysmic passages. Minions of Lamashtu delight in following these titanic horrors, picking over the ruins and bodies of the dead they leave behind.

Variants

The argorth presented here is but the most common variety. As each argorth is the spawn of a Mother of Obvlivion—creatures known for the destructive irregularity of their forms—many exist that possess traits passed on by their horrifying progenitors.

Cinder Scourge: This argorth once terrorized the northern reaches of the Lands of the Linnorm Kings, where—until it vanished in 4699 AR—it was oft mistaken for the malformed offspring of Nidhogg himself. In addition to the abilities of a typical argorth, it possessed immunity to cold, fire resistance 20, and a flaming breath weapon: cloud of smoke and cinders, 60-foot cone, once every 1d4 rounds, damage 14d6, Reflex DC 23 half. The save DC is Constitution-based. An argorth with these abilities has CR +1.

THE CHILDREN OF OBLIVION

It is said that the first argorth were accidental creations of Lamashtu. After many-headed Malcachavka—the first and most bloated of the Mothers of Oblivion—reduced shimmering Operion to little more than a corpse-littered mound of salt, her gore-soaked tentacles, sick with blood fury, refused to let the slaughter end. With nothing living left to lash out at, Malcachavka gnawed and beat upon herself. Six of her largest tentacles—each having claimed thousands of lives that day—were rent and sent thrashing through the air. Where the torn limbs landed they continued to writhe and seek to do slaughter. The mindless rage of each appendage reshaped its form, growing a great maw and many malformed legs. In moments, Malcachavka's rent tentacles rose up and began to feast upon the scattered corpses of Operion. When their perverse anatomies were full and they had each grown large, the abominations scattered, stampedes of worm-like legs propelling each in a separate direction, onward to atrocities of their own. And over fearful Malcachavka and the bloodied sand, Lamashtu watched, awed by her own malevolence, and dubbed these unexpected children of her will argorth, the Children of Oblivion.

MOTHER OF OBLIVION

A monstrous, undulating tangle of barbed tentacles explodes from the water. Its form spurns definable anatomy, a horror of prehistory atop a writhing mass of rubbery tentacles—some crowned with glaring infernal eyes. Its only recognizable feature is the black reptilian head rising above the morass of tentacles, a maw of flesh-sheering teeth gaping wide before two piercing eyes, smoldering with alien intelligence.

MOTHER OF OBLIVION   CR 15

Always CE Gargantuan outsider (aquatic, native)

Init +0; **Senses** all-around vision, darkvision 120 ft.; Listen +22, Spot +30

DEFENSE

AC 32, touch 6, flat-footed 32

  (+26 natural, –4 size)

hp 217 (15d8+150)

Fort +19, **Ref** +9, **Will** +13

DR 15/cold iron and magic; **Immune** death effects, mind-affecting effects, petrification, polymorph; **Resist** acid 20, cold 20; **SR** 26

OFFENSE

Spd 20 ft., swim 60 ft.

Melee bite +24 (2d8+11 plus energy drain) and
  4 tentacles +22 (2d6+6)

Space 20 ft.; **Reach** 20 ft.

Special Attacks breath of madness, constrict 2d6+6, improved grab

Spell-Like Abilities (CL 18)

  At will—*death knell* (DC 17), *invisibility purge, prayer*
  3/day—*demand* (DC 23), *dimensional anchor, divination, dominate person* (DC 20), *greater command* (DC 21)
  1/day—*commune, dream, unhallow*

TACTICS

Before Combat A Mother of Oblivion is rarely surprised. She uses her transdimensional tentacles to keep tabs on the terrain and plan the best ambush.

During Combat Once battle is joined, the Mother of Oblivion uses her breath of madness and energy-draining bite to weaken foes, then merely swats them aside with her Awesome Blow.

Morale A Mother of Oblivion knows no fear, but is wise enough to know when she has lost the advantage. She flees if reduced to fewer than half her hit points.

STATISTICS

Str 37, **Dex** 10, **Con** 31, **Int** 25, **Wis** 18, **Cha** 20

Base Atk +15; **Grp** +40

Feats Awesome Blow, Cleave, Improved Bull Rush, Iron Will, Multiattack, Power Attack

Skills Climb +31, Concentration +28, Escape Artist +18, Hide +26, Intimidate +23, Knowledge (arcana) +25, Knowledge (history) +25, Knowledge (religion) +25, Knowledge (the planes) +25, Listen +22, Move Silently +18, Search +33, Sense Motive +22, Spot +22, Swim +39

Languages Abyssal, Celestial, Common, Draconic, Infernal

SQ transdimensional tentacles

ECOLOGY

Environment any aquatic

Organization solitary

Treasure standard

Advancement 16–30 HD (Gargantuan), 31–45 HD (Colossal)

Level Adjustment —

SPECIAL ABILITIES

All-Around Vision (Ex) The eyes at the tips of several of a Mother of Oblivion's tentacles grant her a +8 racial bonus on Search and Spot checks. She cannot be flanked.

Breath of Madness (Su) A Mother of Oblivion can exhale a cloud of foul-smelling, narcotic breath: 60-foot cone, once per minute, 1d6 points of Wisdom damage and confusion for 1d6 rounds, Reflex DC 27 half Wisdom damage and no confusion. This breath is a mind-affecting poison effect. The save DC is Constitution-based.

Constrict (Ex) A Mother of Oblivion deals 2d6+6 points of damage with a successful grapple check.

Improved Grab (Su) To use this ability, a Mother of Oblivion must hit a creature at least one size category smaller than herself with a tentacle attack. She can then attempt to start a grapple as a free action without provoking an attack of opportunity. If she wins the grapple check, she establishes a hold and can constrict.

Energy Drain (Su) A Mother of Oblivion feeds on soul energy, draining life from her victims. Living creatures hit by a Mother of Oblivion's bite attack gain two negative levels. The DC is 22 for the Fortitude save to remove a negative level. The save DC is Charisma-based. For each such negative level bestowed, the Mother of Oblivion gains 5 temporary hit points.

Transdimensional Tentacles (Su) A Mother of Oblivion's tentacles allow her to see into and infiltrate multiple planes at once. At all times, a Mother of Oblivion is cognisant of the plane she inhabits bodily and all coterminous planes—such as the Ethereal Plane and Plane of Shadow from the Material Plane. Not only is she aware of these planes and the creatures there, she can reach her tentacles through to attack. By worming her tentacles through the dimensions, a Mother of Oblivion can effectively reach through solid barriers into any area not protected by a *dimensional lock* or similar effect. While a Mother of Oblivion can attack and even grapple creatures on other planes, she cannot move creatures from one plane to another.

Warp Dimensions (Su) A Mother of Oblivion's presence distorts the dimensions. Any creature that attempts to utilize a teleport effect within 300 feet of a Mother of Oblivion must make a DC 21 caster level check or the teleport effect fails to activate and the creature must make a DC 27 Fortitude save or be nauseated for 1d6 rounds. The save DC is Constitution-based.

The Mothers of Oblivion are favored servants of Lamashtu, embodiments of the goddess's reign over beasts, monsters, and madness. Unholy augers of her will, all Mothers of Oblivion are meant to confound the works of the civilized world, spread fear of monsters and the wilds, and direct Lamashtu's lesser servants in acts of depravity and bloodshed. It is said the goddess speaks directly to these aquatic terrors and for many, the words of a Mother of Oblivion are equal to the commands of Lamashtu herself.

Bearing a head like a plesiosaur atop a thrashing mass of tentacles and eyes, even the smallest Mothers of Oblivion are more than 30 feet tall—far larger if measured from the head to the farthest tentacle tip. From the watery depths in which they lurk, these horrific masterminds keep constant vigil over multiple planes, watching for both unwary prey and new servants to intimidate into their goddess's service. Immortal beings, Mothers of Oblivion often know much of the past and the languages of civilizations long since fallen.

Ecology

Creatures of chaos and madness, the abominable Mothers of Oblivion are said to have been created by the goddess of monsters to serve as mouthpieces and leaders among her savage minions. Some esoteric texts—sacreligious even to Lamashtu's profane church—claim that the Mothers of Oblivion are actually sisters of Lamashtu, subjugated by the goddess, robbed of their divinity, and cast down to Golarion as her twisted servitors. Whatever their heritage, for uncounted centuries the Mothers of Oblivion have been among the favored servants of Lamashtu and throughout history have risen to mete out her unholy wrath. Rare in the extreme—and despite what the fearful mortal races call them—these monstrosities seem to have no ability to reproduce themselves, though the insane blood furies and rampages they sometimes indulge in have been known to spawn horrors known as argoths (see page 88).

Habitat & Society

Mothers of Oblivion slink in the darkest, deepest reaches of the world, shunning daylight and the gaze of insect-like mortals who would gawk and abandon their pathetic minds at the merest glimpse. The deepest reaches of oceans and the oldest lakes serve as redoubts for these forsaken queens of madness. From these depths, they sate themselves on sea creatures, the offerings of their servants, and the occasional unwary victim dragged screaming from the surface. They are careful to keep their presence secret from those of the world above. From the depths, Mothers of Oblivion form intricate hierarchies of servants and go-betweens, reaching their black tentacles through the societies of amphibious intermediaries into the demesnes of greater monstrosities and the communities of men.

Treasure

Mothers of Oblivion have no need of treasure, but the belongings of their victims often litter the watery depths of their lairs.

THE MYTH OF BLACK MAGGA

Fisherfolk and woodsmen who have ventured near the Storval Depths have long told tales of a fell monster rising from the depths. Below are a few commonly misheld "facts" about Black Magga.

Storm Bringer: Sightings of Black Magga often herald powerful storms and hurricanes. It is said that the beast summons these storms to blow victims into her watery domain.

Blood Tongue: Many who have seen Black Magga and lived to tell the tale can never truly do so. Supposedly, when they attempt to speak of their experience, black blood wells from their mouths, choking their words. Thus, far fewer claim to have seen Black Magga than actually have.

God-Proof: Magga is older than the gods. Divine magic has no effect whatsoever on her abominable form. Anyone who cuts Magga's black heart from her vile chest and bathes in its putrescent blood will likewise become invulnerable to the power of the gods.

OGREKIN

Fleshy and deformed, this man-like cretin hulks far larger and burlier than others of his race. Chunky flesh and overlarge muscles deform his crooked frame, and a dull-witted eagerness shines through jaundiced eyes.

Savage, cruel, and lacking all conscience, ogres typically raid for three reasons: out of greed, for love of slaughter, or—worst of all—to procreate. Fortunate victims of ogre attacks are quickly killed, their bodies turned into morbid playthings. Those who survive such attacks, however, face much worse.

Creating an Ogrekin

"Ogrekin" is a template that can be added to any Medium fey, humanoid, or monstrous humanoid, hereafter referred to as the "base creature."

An ogrekin uses all the base creature's statistics and special abilities except as noted here.

Size and Type: The base creature's type changes to giant. Do not recalculate Hit Dice, base attack bonus, or saves. Size is unchanged, although ogrekin are generally bulkier and taller than the base creature (but not so much that their size increases).

Armor Class: Natural armor bonus increases by +3.

Special Qualities: An ogrekin has the special qualities of the base creature, plus low-light vision.

In addition, all ogrekin are deformed and hideous, and each bears different mutations and ungainly features as gifts from its brutish parent. Roll once on each of the following tables to determine an ogrekin's two deformities—one an advantage, and one a flaw.

d10	Advantageous Deformity
1	*Webbed Digits:* The ogrekin has thick, flexible webbing between its fingers and toes, gaining a swim speed equal to half its base land speed.
2	*Oversized Limb:* The ogrekin can wield weapons one size category larger than normal with no penalty and gains an additional +2 bonus to Strength.
3	*Thick Skin:* The ogrekin has particularly dense skin, callused hide, or layers of blubber that provide additional protection. Increase the ogrekin's natural armor bonus by an additional +2.
4	*Enhanced Senses:* The ogrekin has unusual or extra sensory organs—like a giant eye, lolling tongue, extra ears, or a powerful sense of smell—granting it a +2 bonus on Search and Spot checks.
5	*Triple-Jointed:* The ogrekin's body bends and moves in unsettling ways. It gains a +4 racial bonus on Escape Artist checks and can move through areas half its space in size without squeezing.
6	*Oversized Maw:* The ogrekin's mouth is large and filled with teeth, granting it a bite attack that deals 1d4 points of damage as a secondary natural attack.
7	*Vestigial Limb:* The ogrekin has a vestigial third arm that grants it a +4 racial bonus on grapple checks. The extra limb lacks the strength to wield weapons or shields or the dexterity to perform fine manipulations.
8	*Fierce Visage:* The ogrekin is particularly ferocious and monstrously deformed. It gains a +4 racial bonus on Intimidate checks.
9	*Quick Metabolism:* The ogrekin gains a +2 racial bonus on Fortitude saves and, whenever it rests, it gains double the normal amount of healing.
10	*Vestigial Twin:* A sick little malformed twin (usually a face and one or two limbs) grows off the base creature and acts as a "backup" mind. The ogrekin gains a +2 racial bonus on Will saves and a +2 bonus on any one Knowledge check.

d10	Disadvantageous Deformity
1	*Obese:* The ogrekin is hideously fat and has its Dexterity reduced by 2 (minimum score of 1).
2	*Extra Ugly:* The ogrekin is particularly ugly and foolish looking, taking a –4 penalty on all Charisma-based skill checks.
3	*Light-Sensitive:* The ogrekin's eyes are large and protruding. It is dazzled while in areas of bright sunlight or within the radius of a *daylight* spell.
4	*Weak Mind:* The ogrekin's head is huge and misshapen with rampant bone growth. It takes a –2 penalty on all Will saves.
5	*Speech Impediment:* The ogrekin's mouth and throat are deformed, causing it to slur and stutter. It has difficulty speaking, takes a –2 penalty on all skill checks that rely upon speech, and has a +20% spell failure chance when casting any spell with a verbal component.
6	*Deformed Hand:* One of the ogrekin's hands is deformed. It cannot effectively wield weapons with that hand and takes a –2 penalty on attack rolls with two-handed weapons.
7	*Stunted Legs:* The ogrekin's legs are particularly short and its feet clubfooted. Reduce its base speed by 10 feet (to a minimum of 5 feet).
8	*Pinhead:* The ogrekin's head is comically small. It takes an additional –2 penalty to its Intelligence score.
9	*Fragile:* The ogrekin is a bleeder, has brittle bones, or is particularly frail and gaunt. It loses its normal +4 racial bonus to Constitution.
10	*Freakish Birth:* The ogrekin was born lucky and has no disadvantageous deformity.

Abilities: Change from the base creature as follows: +6 Strength, +4 Constitution, –2 Intelligence, –2 Charisma.

Challenge Rating: Same as the base creature +1.

Alignment: Usually evil.

Level Adjustment: +2.

Sample Ogrekin

Hateful siblings of the grossly inbred Graul family, Maulgro and Lucky are half-human, half-ogre degenerates with the minds of children. Physically, Maulgro has no legs and an oversized mouth full of sharp teeth, while Lucky is triple-jointed. Their statistics, however, are essentially the same, except as noted below.

MAULGRO AND LUCKY GRAUL   CR 3

Male ogrekin human fighter 2

CE Medium humanoid

Init +5; **Senses** low-light vision; Listen +1, Spot +1

DEFENSE

AC 18, touch 11, flat-footed 17

    (+4 armor, +1 Dex, +3 natural)

hp 23 (2d10+8)

Fort +7, **Ref** +1, **Will** +1

OFFENSE

Spd 30 ft. (Lucky) or 20 ft. (Maulgro)

Melee unarmed strike +8 (1d3+5) and

    bite +2 (1d6+2, Maulgro only)

TACTICS

Before Combat These ogrekin lack the foresight or intellect to do anything useful in preparation for battle. Rather, they spend the moments before an impending battle hurling crude curses at one another, working themselves into a rage.

During Combat These two ogrekin hate each other and don't fight together. Each tries to keep his own foe to himself, and each time the other is critically hit (or even killed), the other takes a move action to laugh at the misfortune of his brother.

Morale These ogrekin have little concept yet of death, and as such fight to the bitter end.

STATISTICS

Str 20, **Dex** 13, **Con** 19, **Int** 8, **Wis** 12, **Cha** 6

Base Atk +2; **Grp** +7

Feats Improved Initiative, Improved Grapple, Improved Unarmed Strike, Weapon Focus (unarmed strike)

Skills Climb +10, Escape Artist +1 (+5 for Lucky), Swim +10

Languages Giant

Gear hide shirt

SPECIAL ABILITIES

Maulgro's Deformities (Ex) Maulgro has an oversized mouth filled with sharp teeth, and stunted legs that hardly work—his preferred method of moving around is to walk on his hands and drag his stumps along behind him.

Lucky's Deformities (Ex) Lucky's limbs bend strangely—he's triple-jointed. He has no disadvantageous deformity.

Ogrekin Clans

Too small and flimsy to be taken in by their ogre progenitors, and treated as outcasts and monsters by their other parent's race, ogrekin tend to form small, brutish, and often inbred clans, living off the scraps of ogres and other savage giants or preying upon weaker races. While the Grauls are detailed in "The Hook Mountain Massacre," other families of ogrekin can be found throughout Golarion.

    Beane: High on the cliffs outside the town of Torcova lies the manor of Lord Sauton Beane. What none in the town below know is that their benevolent lordship is an abnormally

handsome ogrekin, blessed with no deformities except for a sixth toe on each foot. Eager for an heir, Lord Beane has taken seven wives, but each has given birth to a truly monstrous ogrekin. Having murdered each wife for her uterine betrayal, Lord Beane keeps his deformed sons locked away in the caves beneath his manor, loosing them only to punish his enemies or to claim his next wife.

    The Shouk: In the mountains of Thuvia live the insular oracles known as the Shouk. Centuries ago, ogreblood tainted the line of holy men, and each generation since has yielded more and more depraved and cannibalistic brutes, now completely devoid of prophetic ability. Out of tradition, though, tribes still come to the Shouk in their times of need, seeking advice but often losing several members in the effort.

    The Sons of Rovagug: This clan of massive ogrekin dominates the Flesh Pens of Urglin, murdering all comers in the fierce underground gladiatorial battles. All seven members are actually female, having mutilated their overly fleshy bodies to appear as men.

VALEROS

MALE HUMAN FIGHTER 7

ALIGN NG **INIT** +7 **SPEED** 20 ft.

DEITY Cayden Cailean **HOMELAND** Andoran

ABILITIES

16	STR
16	DEX
12	CON
13	INT
8	WIS
10	CHA

DEFENSE

HP 50

AC 20
touch 13, flat-footed 17

Fort +6, **Ref** +5, **Will** +1

OFFENSE

Melee +1 frost longsword +12/+7 (1d8+6/19–20 plus 1d6 cold) or
+1 frost longsword +10/+5 (1d8+6/19–20 plus 1d6 cold) and
+1 short sword +10 (1d6+2/19–20)
Ranged mwk comp longbow +11/+6 (1d8+3/×3)
Base Atk +7; **Grp** +10

SKILLS

Climb	+10
Intimidate	+10
Ride	+13
Swim	+7

FEATS

Big Game Hunter[B], Combat Expertise, Improved Initiative, Power Attack, Two-Weapon Defense, Two-Weapon Fighting, Weapon Focus (longsword), Weapon Focus (short sword), Weapon Specialization (longsword)

Combat Gear alchemist's fire (2), elixir of fire breath, potion of bear's endurance, potion of cure moderate wounds (3); **Other Gear** +1 breastplate, +1 frost longsword, +1 short sword, mwk composite longbow (+3 Str) with 20 arrows, silver dagger, gauntlets of ogre power, backpack, lucky tankard, rations (6), 50 ft. silk rope, 30 pp, 17 gp

Born a farmer's son in the quiet Andorian countryside, Valeros spent his youth dreaming of adventure and exploring the world. For the past several years, he's done exactly that, having been a mercenary with the Band of the Mauler, a guard for the Aspis Consortium, a freelance bounty hunter, and hired muscle for a dozen different employers in as many lands. Gone is his youthful naivete, replaced by scars and the resolve of a veteran warrior. Although he possesses a keen wit, he finds the simplest, most direct approach is often the best, and has little patience for convoluted schemes or magical chicanery. While noble at heart, Valeros hides this beneath a jaded, sometimes crass demeanor, often claiming that there's no better way to end a day's adventuring than with "an evening of hard drinking and a night of soft company."

SEONI

FEMALE HUMAN SORCERER 7

ALIGN LN **INIT** +2 **SPEED** 30 ft.

DEITY Pharasma **HOMELAND** Varisia

ABILITIES

8	STR
14	DEX
12	CON
10	INT
13	WIS
18	CHA

DEFENSE

HP 26

AC 15
touch 14, flat-footed 13

Fort +3, **Ref** +4, **Will** +6

OFFENSE

Melee quarterstaff +2 (1d6–1)
Ranged mwk dagger +6 (1d4–1/19–20)
Base Atk +3; **Grp** +2

Spells Known (CL 7th, 8th with evocation; +5 ranged touch)
3rd (5/day)—haste, lightning bolt (DC 19)
2nd (7/day)—invisibility, scorching ray, web
1st (7/day)—burning hands (DC 17), enlarge person, mage armor, magic missile, shield
0 (6/day)—acid splash, daze (DC 14), detect magic, light, mage hand, prestidigitation, read magic
Spell-Like Abilities (CL 7th)
1/day—dancing lights

SKILLS

Bluff	+14
Climb	+2
Concentration	+11
Listen	+3
Spellcraft	+10
Spot	+3

FEATS

Alertness (when Dragon is in reach), Dodge, Extend Spell, Greater Spell Focus (evocation), Spell Focus (evocation), Varisian Tattoo (evocation)[B]

FAMILIAR

Dragon (blue-tailed skink: as lizard, MM 275)

Combat Gear potion of cure moderate wounds, scroll of fireball, scroll of fly, tanglefoot bag, wand of magic missile (CL 3rd, 50 charges); **Other Gear** mwk dagger, quarterstaff, amulet of natural armor +1, cloak of Charisma +2, ring of protection +2, handy haversack, everburning torch, rations (4), 20 pp, 34 gp

Despite being a consummate adventurer, Seoni is something of an enigma to her compatriots. Quietly neutral on most matters, bound by codes and mandates that she rarely feels compelled to explain, the sorceress keeps her emotions tightly bottled. Extremely detail-oriented—a trait that has led Merisiel to often call her a "control freak"—Seoni is a careful and meticulous planner, a schemer who frequently finds herself frustrated by the improvised plans of her more impulsive companions. Despite all of this, Seoni has stuck by her comrades through numerous tight spots, a fact that continues to amaze and confuse Valeros, who often wonders loudly (although not altogether unappreciatively) about "the witch and her schemes."

MERISIEL

FEMALE ELF ROGUE 7

ALIGN CN   **INIT** +5   **SPEED** 30 ft.

DEITY Calistria   **HOMELAND** Absalom

ABILITIES

12	STR
20	DEX
12	CON
8	INT
13	WIS
10	CHA

DEFENSE

HP 34

AC 20
touch 15, flat-footed 15

Fort +3, Ref +11, Will +3
(+5 against enchantment)

Defense evasion, trap sense +2, uncanny dodge; **Immune** sleep

OFFENSE

Melee +1 keen rapier +11 (1d6+2/15–20)
Ranged dagger +10 (1d4+1/19–20)
Base Atk +5; **Grp** +6

Special Attack sneak attack +4d6

SKILLS

Bluff	+10
Disable Device	+9
Hide	+10
Jump	+16
Listen	+9
Move Silently	+10
Open Lock	+12
Search	+7
Sleight of Hand	+12
Spot	+11
Tumble	+13

FEATS

City Born[B], Dodge, Mobility, Weapon Finesse

 Combat Gear potion of cure moderate wounds (2), potion of invisibility (2); **Other Gear** +1 studded leather armor, +1 keen rapier, daggers (12), amulet of natural armor +1, gloves of Dexterity +2, ring of jumping, rations (3), masterwork thieves' tools, polished jade worth 50 gp, 70 pp

Merisiel's life experiences have taught her to enjoy things to their fullest as they occur, since it's impossible to tell when the good times might end. Just over a century old—still an adolescent as her people count age— she's already grown used to watching her friends grow old. She's open and expressive with her thoughts and emotions, and never hesitates to make them known when things go wrong. Never the sharpest knife in the drawer, Merisiel makes up for this by carrying at least a dozen of them on her person. She hasn't met a problem yet that can't, in one way or another, be solved with things that slice. While she's always on the move and working on her latest batch of plots for easy money, in the end it comes down to being faster than everyone else—either on her feet, or with her beloved blades. She wouldn't have it any other way.

KYRA

FEMALE HUMAN CLERIC 7

ALIGN NG   **INIT** –1   **SPEED** 20 ft.

DEITY Sarenrae   **HOMELAND** Qadira

ABILITIES

13	STR
8	DEX
14	CON
10	INT
18	WIS
12	CHA

DEFENSE

HP 49

AC 20
touch 10, flat-footed 20

Fort +8, Ref +2, Will +13

OFFENSE

Melee +1 scimitar +8 (1d6+2/18–20)
Ranged light crossbow +4 (1d8/19–20)
Base Atk +5; **Grp** +6
Special Attacks greater turning 1/day, turn undead 4/day (+3, 2d6+8)
Spells Prepared (CL 7th, +4 ranged touch)
4th—divine power, fire shield[D], restoration
3rd—blindness/deafness (DC 17), dispel magic, remove disease, searing light[D]
2nd—aid, bull's strength, heat metal[D] (DC 16), resist energy, spiritual weapon
1st—bless, command (DC 15), cure light wounds[D], divine favor, sanctuary (DC 15), shield of faith
0—detect magic (2), light, mending (2), read magic

D domain spell; **Domains** healing, sun

SKILLS

Concentration	+12
Heal	+14
Knowledge (religion)	+10

FEATS

Combat Casting, Country Born[B], Iron Will, Martial Weapon Proficiency (scimitar), Weapon Focus (scimitar)

 Combat Gear holy water (3), wand of cure moderate wounds (40 charges); **Other Gear** +2 chainmail, +1 heavy steel shield, +1 scimitar, light crossbow with 20 bolts, cloak of resistance +1, periapt of Wisdom +2, ring of protection +1, backpack, gold holy symbol (with continual flame) worth 300 gp, rations (4), 30 pp

Kyra was one of the few survivors of a brutal raid on her hometown, and on the smoking ruins of her village she swore her life and sword arm to Sarenrae. Possessed of a fierce will, pride in her faith, and skill with the scimitar, Kyra has traveled far since her trial by fire. She lost her family and home that fateful day, yet where another might be consumed by anger and a thirst for revenge, Kyra has found peace in the Dawnflower, and in the belief that, if she can prevent even one death at evil hands, her own losses will not have been in vain. While her faith runs deep, she does not see herself as an evangelist and saves her sermonizing for those with ears to hear her enlightenment—a virtue largely learned after many frustrating philosophical arguments with Merisiel and Valeros.

NEXT MONTH IN PATHFINDER

FORTRESS OF THE STONE GIANTS

by Wolfgang Baur

The giants are on the march! Threatening rumors take deadly form when the vanguard of an army of stone giant warriors descends on Sandpoint! Can the PCs hope to defend the peaceful community from foes more than double their size? And what of the army gathering in the mountains and the plots of its nefarious general?

DRAGONS OF GOLARION

by Mike McArtor

Dragons both chromatic and metallic clash in the skies of the Pathfinder Chronicles campaign setting. Learn of their history, ways, rivalries, and everything else you need to bring these wyrms to life.

BORN OF STONE

by Wolfgang Baur

Their epics etched upon the faces of mountains, stone giants tower over the puny civilized races. Discover the details of their ancient culture and learn what strife might lead these titans to war.

PATHFINDER'S JOURNAL

Robbed! Pathfinder Eando Kline visits Sirathu and becomes the target of a band of fleet-footed filchers. His pursuit leads him all the way to Korvosa, the Jewel of Varisia, and reveals a plot more sinister than he ever expected.

BESTIARY

Cast-iron devils, giant giants, shining sons of madness, beings "lean and athirst," and worse!

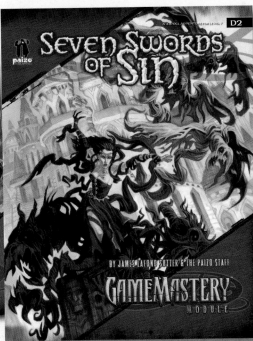
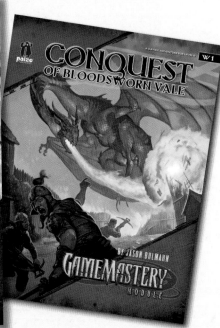

Find Your Path.

Look for these upcoming Pathfinder releases :

Pathfinder Rise of the Runelords Players Guide (5-Pack)
PZO9000 $9.99   Available now!

Pathfinder #2 Rise of the Runelords: The Skinsaw Murders
PZO9002 $19.99   September 2007

Pathfinder #3 Rise of the Runelords: The Hook Mountain Massacre
PZO9003 $19.99   October 2007

Pathfinder #4 Rise of the Runelords: Fortress of the Stone Giants
PZO9004 $19.99   November 2007

Pathfinder #5 Rise of the Runelords: Sins of the Saviors
PZO9005 $19.99   December 2007

Pathfinder #6 Rise of the Runelords: Spires of Xin-Shalast
PZO9006 $19.99   January 2008